AURA GARDEN GUIDES

Siegfried Stein

Perennials

AURA BOOKS

Aura Garden Guides

Perennials

Siegfried Stein

Original German language edition:
Gärten leicht und richtig
Sommerblumen
© 1994 BLV Verlagsgesellschaft
mbH, München, Germany

This edition produced by:
Transedition Limited for
Aura Books, Bicester
and first published in 2002

English language edition
© 1995 Advanced Marketing (UK) Ltd.,
Bicester, England

English language translation by:
Andrew Shackleton for Translate-A-Book,
a division of Transedition Ltd.,
Oxford

Typesetting by:
Organ Graphic, Abingdon

10 9 8 7 6 5 4 3 2 1
Printed in Dubai

ISBN 1 903938 00 7

Photographic credits
All photographs by the author,
except: Morell 42/43, 46/47, 47 top;
Photos Horticultural 10; Reinhard
44/45, 51; Seidl 92/93, 95; Suttons
Seeds 11. Cover photographs: Harry
Smith (front); Bildarchiv Gitte (back
left); E. Morell (back right)

CONTENTS

Foreword

Paradise is depicted as a garden. In it, flowers, fruits, animals and people flourish in peace and mutual harmony.

The image of a green oasis like this, rich with flowers, occurs in almost all the cultures of the ancient world. Between the Euphrates and the Tigris, and in Persia and in Israel, such a garden of plenty must have been a stark contrast to their own hostile and barren surroundings, where the scorching heat of the sun transformed the land into desert.

Our gardens are a great deal more like those dream pictures of our ancestors. A temperate climate with plentiful rain provides good growing conditions for plants, allowing flowers to flourish almost everywhere. From early spring until far into the winter, we can all appreciate the colours, shapes and scents that our flowers have to offer us.

For the plants, all that beauty isn't just an end in itself; it also helps to preserve the species and to provide food for animals. A favourable climate, without violent extremes of cold and heat, or rain and drought, offers us great abundance; when we intervene, we should do so with care.

Many of the countries of Europe have a long tradition of flower-growing. Where else, for example, do the window boxes and balconies spill over in a riot of colour? Where else is there space among the flowering perennials for the many colourful summer flowers that have found their way to us from all over the world?

There's always something new to admire and try out. The breeders are developing new varieties and colours. Variegated shades are in strong demand, but loud and gaudy colours are still providing highlights, though nowadays they've retreated into the background a little. And people are still continuing to discover entirely new flowers — flowers that can totally change the look of even the most colourful garden.

No wonder gardening never loses its fascination.

Yours,

Siegfried Stein

A colourful crowd of summer flowers

Designing with plants

If you have plenty of room in your garden, count yourself lucky. Even so, not everybody wants to be completely absorbed in their garden. Some people prefer to have it as a pleasant place to relax, without having to work too hard at it.

If that's what *you* want, split up a large garden into low-mainten-ance zones (for instance a flower meadow, or a moist zone with a pond), and into areas with ground cover, bushes, shrubs and trees where nature is pretty much left to itself. Your romantic view certainly won't be spoiled by a controlled wilderness area. Of course, looking after herba-ceous borders, beds planted with summer flowers, and the pots and containers around the house takes a little more work.

Gardens always betray some-thing of the character of their owners. Romantics tend to prefer a profusion of flowers, perhaps with nothing more than box hedges to keep them in shape, or sections separated by bricks, hedges or walls. Others place more importance on well-ordered surroundings. They ensure that the soil conditions and the situation are absolutely right, and so create an environ-ment where even unusual specimens can develop.

You can also design your garden — or at least parts of it — for minimal maintenance. Use grasses, pebbles and paved surfaces. Put down bark as a mulch, and use ground-cover plants or slow-growing trees and shrubs. This doesn't stop your garden producing a profusion of flowers, with long-lasting herba-ceous perennials like marguerites (*Leucanthemum vulgare*), garden loosestrife (*Lysimachia congesti-flora, L. punctata*), phlox and asters, with bulbs like narcissi, tulips, lilies and autumn crocuses (*Colchicum autumnale*) and with wild flower mixtures. These can be sown in open spaces, and produce flowers constantly from June till the frosts.

In broad, open gardens, there isn't much to catch the eye. Create a natural boundary with embankments, or subdivide the garden to create smaller, more intimate 'garden rooms'. Hedges should be evergreen as far as possible; choose yew, privet, box, juniper, American arbor-vitae (or white cedar, *Thuja occidentalis*) or cherry laurel (*Prunus laurocerasus*). You can also make hedges with flowering shrubs like forsythia, weigela, berberis and firethorn (*Pyracan-tha*). For a backdrop that also gives protection from the wind, plant a mixture of ornamental trees and bushes — or think about wooden sight-screens, frames for climbing plants, pergolas, palings or walls. Any of these will show the colours and shapes of the flowers to their best advantage.

A 'garden room' like this can be a corner where you sit to catch the morning or evening sun. It can house a herb garden. It can shelter wind-sensitive perennials. With a dry-stone

Perennials line the edge of this path, providing an attractive blend of colours.

grow determine how a garden will develop. A sunny plot of land will quickly become dark as the trees start to grow, checking the growth of perennials and annuals. Right from the start, make allowances for the size of the mature trees, and plant them an appropriate distance from boundaries. You'll often be better served by smaller shrubs and trees. And don't restrict yourself to a single example of each species and variety; plant several. That ensures harmony and makes the whole scheme look more generous.

The classic planting scheme has low, spreading annuals and perennials in the foreground, with medium-sized plants of bushy habit behind them and tall plants clearly visible above them at the back.

A meadow-like planting style can introduce variety and a delicate, hazy effect; here taller inflorescences, planted singly or in groups, stand out above a low carpet of flowers, much as they do in the wild.

Incidentally, most of those perfect-looking garden arrangements were unsuccessful first time around. There's nearly always one plant, at least, that doesn't turn out too well and needs to be replaced. So it's a good thing there are plenty of fast-growing and inexpensive summer bedding plants to fill up those gaps!

wall, it can become a sun-trap for tender plants. You can make it into a water garden, furnish it with container plants or decorate it with artistic elements. Gardens designed around a theme or a colour are also popular, with white, pink, blue, blue-white or yellow and red combinations of perennials and summer flowers.

And don't forget the trees. Their size and the way they

7

Colours to brighten up a garden

For centuries, painters and artists have been busy studying the effects of different colours. Johann Wolfgang von Goethe, a keen plant enthusiast, developed a colour circle for use in the garden. And Gertrude Jekyll, one of the best-known English artists of the garden and a specialist in perennials, transferred her art to garden design; she was developing her ideas in the first third of this century. Her garden style and her cleverly devised planting plans, the product of years of work, still distinguish many famous English gardens today.

She also devised the 'monochrome' garden, in which plants whose leaves and flowers have the same or similar colours are planted together. Tonal plantings can have a very elegant

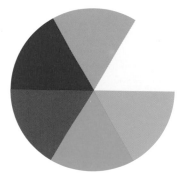

The colour wheel shows which colours work well together.

effect, though it isn't essential to design large areas of the garden in this way. Smaller combinations, based round one larger or long-flowering main plant, can also be effective.

The colour wheel shows the *complementary* colours: these are the ones that appear opposite one another. Thus red complements green, one colour heightening the effect of the other. Blue goes just as well with orange, and pure yellow with purple. If you put an equilateral triangle into the colour circle, you can find the appropriate supplementary colour.

Groups of cold or warm colours, which have a shade in common and lie next to each other in the colour wheel, can also have a pleasing effect. Combinations of this kind lack excitement, but they do look harmonious.

So there are several possible combinations. You can link cold colours like a blue shade of purple-red (but not brilliant orange-red) with violet and blue, or warm colours (like scarlet) with all the shades of orange and yellow. Single spots of a completely different colour — for example, a few blooms in

Shades of red and blue look good together; white heightens the effect.

white — will heighten the effect, and bring a planting scheme to life.

Each colour is thought to have its own particular characteristics.

Red is seen as exciting and fiery, the warm, cheering colour of summer. Red flowers look as if they're closer to you than blue ones; blue flowers tend to give breadth and distance to a garden, so they can make small gardens look bigger.

Blue has a cool, calming effect, but it can also be unusual and attention-grabbing. Look, for example, at the sky-blue delphinium, the delicate flax (*Linum*), or the brilliant blue

hound's tongue (*Anchusa azurea*). The combination of blue and white is very lively and fresh; the addition of green tones produces a calming effect.

White is one of the most important elements in the garden. It lifts the other colours, making them look clearer and more brilliant, and neutralises competing shades. That's partic ularly true of the closely related silver-white on leaves, stalks and fruits; this can create an impres- sion of dryness, and of simul- taneous warmth and coolness.

Yellow brings sunshine into the garden. On rainy days, in particular, it sets a cheerful,

*Harmony of colours and contours: brownish-red sneezeweed (*Heleni- um*) and yellow gloriosa daisies (*Rudbeckia*)

carefree mood. It goes well with orange, brilliant red and shades of brown. And a strong yellow makes a really good contrast to violet, blue and white. There's a wide choice of yellow flowers available in all shades, so it won't be too difficult to find suitable partners.

Planting schemes in related colours create a feeling of harmony that induces a nostal- gic, romantic mood. Contrasts, on the other hand, look invig- orating, and create a lively and interesting effect. But don't plant shades of more than three basic colours together, or you'll find that everything will tend to look overloaded.

Diversity from seeds

It's well worth raising your own summer flowers in the garden frame or greenhouse, or if need be on the window sill. Besides, many of them need so little attention that you can sow them where they're going to flower.

You'll find a huge choice of interesting species and varieties available as seeds, though as in fashion there are constant changes. As well as old, well-tried species and varieties, you'll find more and more wild flowers for naturalistic gardens and low-maintenance seed mixtures. These colourful plants provide pollen and nectar for beneficial insects like bees, bumble bees and butterflies.

Asters, annual chrysanthemum (*Chrysanthemum carinatum*), love-in-a-mist (*Nigella damascena*), gloriosa daisy (*Rudbeckia hirta*), *Clarkia*, nasturtium (*Tropaeolum majus*), godetia (*Godetia grandiflora*), Californian poppy (*Eschscholzia californica*) and corn poppy (*Papaver rhoeas*), mallow (*Lavatera trimestris*) and annual sunflower (*Helianthus annuus*) — like the wild flowers, none of these needs to be started under glass. In spring (May at the latest) sow them outside in shallow drills, in a sunny seed-bed that has been worked to a fine tilth. The distance between rows should be approximately 6 in (15 cm); you transplant the seedlings later, complete with their little root balls.

It's even simpler to sow direct. Just scatter the seeds as thinly as possible, either in drills around ¾ in (1.5-2 cm) deep or broadcast between the perennials, where the plants will flower. Cover them lightly with fine soil and water thoroughly. When they are 1½-2½ in (4-6 cm) tall, thin them out to their final spacing so they have room to grow.

Pelargoniums, petunias, snapdragons (*Antirrhinum majus*) and many other summer flowers need to be started under cover. In the warm, under protecting glass, scatter the seeds thinly and evenly in pans or pots filled with a free-draining, sterile seed compost. Firm the compost gently with a board so that the seeds make contact with the soil, sieve a layer of sand or seed compost around 1/8 in (2-4 mm) deep over them, and water thoroughly with a fine rose.

If you use garden compost, you must sterilise it first to kill any pathogens. Put it in a heat-resistant tray or foil and heat it in the oven at 300°F (150°C, or gas mark 2) for about 30 minutes. Mix a little grit or sharp sand with the compost for drainage.

To stop the seeds drying out as they germinate, put the tray in a heated propagator, or cover it with a propagator lid or even a transparent plastic sheet. Make sure it's kept warm enough — 61-68°F (16-20°C) is usually

A comprehensive selection of pots and trays for raising seedlings

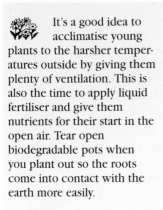

It's a good idea to acclimatise young plants to the harsher temperatures outside by giving them plenty of ventilation. This is also the time to apply liquid fertiliser and give them nutrients for their start in the open air. Tear open biodegradable pots when you plant out so the roots come into contact with the earth more easily.

enough — and the seedlings will soon appear.

When the first true leaves (i.e. not the seed-leaves) have developed, the seedlings should be carefully pricked out (transferred), ideally into a modular unit with individual plastic cells (but you can also use trays, yoghurt pots or pots made from clay, plastic or recycled paper).

To prick out, use a widger to lift out the seedlings; take care not to touch the roots. Put each

Top left: *Evenly distributed, and not too thick — that's how the seed should fall.*

Above: *Even so soon after germination, the seedlings already need more room.*

There's always an empty space among the perennials where you can sow summer flowers.

seedling individually into a hole you've made for it. Using the widger, press earth against it from both sides. Don't put these delicate little plants too deeply into the ground: the seed-leaves should still be visible above soil level. Water with a fine rose and put the plants somewhere that's warm enough for them to grow on until they're ready for planting out. They'll need light, but avoid bright sunlight.

The delicate seedlings will dry out more slowly — and they'll germinate and grow better — if you cover the seed bed or drills with fleece, perforated film, cloches or a portable garden frame. This creates a sheltered nursery that is moist and warm. Don't forget to label your plants with details such as botanical name, variety and date of sowing.

Division, cuttings, runners, root cuttings

Division

With perennials, tubers, root-tubers and rhizomes, division is the quickest and simplest propagation method. Often the clumps themselves are trying to grow apart, and you can see where your spade will split them with the least possible damage. You don't divide plants when they're in full growth, which means you should do it only in autumn, on frost-free days in winter, or in spring up to the beginning of May. There are some exceptions. Plants like the common flag iris (*Iris germanica*), for instance, have their dormant period after flowering and then start back into growth.

Dig up the clump with a fork or spade, pierce the root-ball through the middle, and pull it apart. Sometimes you can do this with your hands. More often the only way to do it is with a sharp spade, pressed down firmly with your foot. You can divide the root balls into as many sections as you like, but each section must always retain at least one shoot, and preferably more. Plant the sections in their new positions without delay, at the same depth as before, and water them in thoroughly.

Mat-forming perennials like *Sedum*, *Aster dumosus* and *Arabis caucasica* spread by means of short shoots. These quickly develop roots while they're still on the main plant. Tear off the little sections with roots and pot them up or replant them. *Sedum* species in this state can be used to provide green cover for a roof; just scatter them, cover them with a bit of earth, and they'll start growing straight away.

Runners

If the shoots are longer, for instance on ground-cover plants like ornamental strawberry (*Fragaria* or *Duchesnea*), periwinkle (*Vinca minor*), foamflower (*Tiarella cordifolia*), *Omphalodes verna* and bugle (*Ajuga reptans*), then gardeners call them runners. Separate rooted sections of the plant and replant them.

Root cuttings

Many plants with long and fleshy roots can't be divided. But their roots have the ability

Rejuvenate your clumps of perennials — divide them!

Summer's the best time to divide iris rhizomes.

Busy Lizzie (Impatiens walleriana) roots easily in a glass of water.

to activate dormant buds, and if you put them in a pot or little box with seed compost, they can develop new plants from the buds.

Good examples of this are Japanese anemone (*Anemone × hybrida*), perennial poppy, *Primula* species, comfrey (*Symphytum officinale*) and sea holly (*Eryngium*).

Lift the parent plant in the autumn, cut off suitable roots and divide them into 1¼–2½ in (3–6 cm) long sections. When you do this, you need to be sure that you can plant the roots the right way up later on, so make the top cut straight and the bottom one sloping. Keeping the roots vertical, put them into little boxes with a sandy soil mixture. If they're kept cool but frost-free, fine new roots and shoots will form.

Cuttings

It's easy to propagate many perennials using non-woody tip or stem cuttings. With some plants (e.g. chrysanthemums and dahlias), new roots will form after just three or four weeks in a 1:1 mixture of peat and sand. The best time to propagate most perennials is in summer, but you can start early in the season.

Start by choosing shoots about 2 in (5 cm) long with two or three pairs of leaves. They should still be soft, but mustn't be weak or leggy.

Fill a largish pot, a pan or a modular tray with clean cutting compost, moisten it and firm it with a board or the back of your hand.

Take your cutting with a quick, clean cut across under a node (leaf joint). Remove the lower pairs of leaves, and trim off half of each of the remaining leaves.

Now plant the cuttings about ½ in (1 cm) deep. Plant them

sufficiently far apart that they aren't touching each other. Using your fingers, draw the compost up around them from both sides, and then firm the cuttings in.

Next use a fine rose on your watering can to water everything thoroughly. Then surround it all with an airtight transparent cover (such as a plastic bag, for instance) to stop it drying out.

Put the cuttings somewhere light but out of direct sunshine; at temperatures of 59–68°F (15–20°C) they'll soon start to form roots.

After three to six weeks, you can see if you've been successful. If the cuttings have rooted, pot them up into fairly nutrient-rich compost and grow them on until they're ready to be planted out.

The right spot for each species

Annual and biennial summer flowers are short-lived, but adapt themselves to most conditions; you don't usually get problems with unsuitable soils.

This means you can use marigolds (*Calendula officinalis*), bellflowers (*Campanula medium*), China asters (*Callistephus chinensis*), zinnias or even the imposing foxgloves (*Digitalis purpurea*) just about anywhere in order to plug a gap or to bring colour into parts of the garden that would otherwise be rather dreary. As long as you consider their basic requirements, they'll fit in nicely with the surrounding trees, bushes and perennials.

Most summer flowers and perennials can cope with a 'good garden soil' — a loose-structured growing medium that isn't water-logged, and has a normal level of lime, a humus content of between 1·5 and 4 per cent and, perhaps, a proportion of sand or gravel. Only a few species will need bog conditions (with an acid, peat soil) or are *calcicoles* (i.e. decidedly lime-loving).

Even so, the soil must be evenly moist for the plants to achieve their fullest growth. Annual flowers can't cope with longer periods of stress; most are put into the soil as plants, and don't have large root systems.

So what can you do? Rather than waiting for trouble, you can enrich the soil with plenty of humus (compost, bark humus, and material produced by recycling) and with nutrients in a form that the plants can easily assimilate.

Mulch laid between the beds can also be a great help in looking after them. A layer of grass-cuttings a good inch (3–4 cm) deep, wood chippings on the paths and around the plants, chopped straw or bark all keep the soil damp for longer and do much to suppress weed growth.

Most annuals and biennials need as much light as possible for as long as possible, so try to put these plants in sunny positions. There are some (but only a few) that also flourish in the shade, such as the mound-forming busy Lizzies (*Impatiens walleriana*), the delicate begonias and *Digitalis purpurea*, which reaches for the heights. Pelargoniums can achieve amazing things: although they originally came from South Africa, and are more accustomed to hot and dry conditions, they can also thrive in shady and difficult parts of the garden.

The long-lived perennials are very much more demanding.

This is hardly surprising, as they have to cope with their particular situation far longer, and hold their own against any nearby shrubs and trees. These put pressure on their roots and draw off nutrients and moisture. The perennials are also growing in competition with each other. As a result, plants that are in a poor

*Red corn poppies (*Papaver rhoeas)* combined with feverfew (*Tanacetum parthenium)*

situation won't survive the cold season as well as their rivals, and will then suffer so much in competition with their luxuriantly sprouting neighbours that they gradually disappear.

This is simply natural selection in action; you can't avoid it completely, no matter how carefully you plan your garden.

Many perennials, such as the well-known *Leucanthemum vulgare*, spread themselves in the garden. They can't endure their original situation for long because of the residues they themselves leave in the soil, which apparently have a bad effect on them. Don't try to curb their wanderlust; just dig them

up every three years, divide them and replant them somewhere else.

If you look in the plant profiles towards the end of the book you'll find specific advice about the conditions most suitable for each of the perennials. With new garden layouts, in particular, you have a chance to improve the

soil conditions, and so ensure that your plants will grow happily for many years.

Sandy soils can be made to hold together better and retain more water if you add plenty of well-rotted organic material, e.g. farmyard manure or garden compost. Composted bark and spent mushroom compost are also good soil conditioners, although the latter will make the soil slightly alkaline.

You can improve drainage in heavy, poorly draining soils by adding coarse gravel or sharp sand, and, of course, by breaking them up deep down. Apply organic mulches frequently to increase the humus and nutrient content of any soil; you can also add well-rotted animal manure and garden compost.

When you're choosing plants, it's generally best to take the soil you've actually got into account. If you begin by testing your soil with one of the cheap kits available from all garden centres, you'll know exactly where you stand. The kits usually tell you how to modify your soil to produce the best results.

Dried blood gives a quick boost to nitrogen levels, while hoof-and-horn and well-rotted animal manure (also available in dried form) work over a longer period. Bonemeal improves the supply of phosphorus, which is responsible for flower formation, and naturally occurring potash can give vital help with root formation and improve the intensity of the flower colours.

Many plants such as *Dianthus* benefit from a limy soil. If you are planning to grow this kind of plant, check your soil with a testing kit first. If you need to add lime, it's available in several forms from your gardening centre. Use it with care, though: you can't grow lime-hating plants such as rhododendrons and heathers in the treated soil, so work on selected areas only.

Slow-release inorganic fertilisers release their nutrients over a period of many weeks, or allow

Iris and poppy complement one another admirably.

roots to take up just as much as they need. Using them avoids the risk of over-fertilising, or of scorching your plants by giving them too much mineral salt. The soil must generally be well loosened before planting.

A rock garden needs gravel, stone chippings, grit or broken bricks in the subsoil to ensure that water drains off quickly.

Similar requirements apply to the dry garden and the wild garden. Here sand and gravel help to make the soil less rich.

You can simulate heath and moorland conditions by adding generous amounts of peat and composted bark; composted pine needles can also be used.

Shaded areas, in particular, need plenty of humus. Leaf mould, garden compost, or composted organic waste (spent hops, for example), are all suitable for enriching the soil.

An ornamental garden, on the other hand, doesn't just need a humus-rich, loosely structured growing medium; it will also require applications of compost, well-rotted animal manure and organic fertiliser. The compost should be applied every year in late winter. Use a bucketful for every square yard/metre — this will give a thin layer around ¼ in (0.5-1 cm) deep.

Preparing the ground thoroughly will give you the chance to rid

Every place is taken in this garden full of perennials.

yourself of problem weeds such as bindweed (*Convolvulus*), ground elder (*Aegopodium podagraria*) and creeping twitch (*Agropyron repens*). The only way to achieve this is by sheer hard physical work — you'll need to dig the soil over thoroughly, going through it and picking out even the smallest bits of weed. If you don't do the job properly, you'll soon discover that the wild plants take the nutrients, water, wind and sun away from your prize specimens and get the upper hand.

Planting is fun

The best months for planting perennials are March, April, September and October, the months when there's little risk of drought. Grasses and ferns should only be planted in spring: if you plant them in autumn they don't form strong roots, so they're in danger of drying out and getting frosted right through the winter. The same goes for autumn-flowering perennials such as chrysanthemums, lobelias (*Lobelia erinus*), *Coreopsis*, autumn anemones (*Anemone × hybrida*) and Michaelmas daisies. Flowers planted in spring won't get as much of a check to their growth in autumn, and can still gather strength for flowering.

For annuals the best time to plant is between the end of April and the beginning of June; for biennials, it's September (or the beginning of October, at the latest) so they can develop good roots well before the first frost.

If gaps *do* appear you can easily fill them, even in high summer, with annuals that have been sown later than the main batch. Some fibrous-rooted plants (e.g. Michaelmas daisies) can be moved in full flower, as long as you soak them thoroughly with water before and after. Raise them in the vegetable garden and use them to replace plants that have finished flowering. Pot-grown perennials are usually too small or spindly to

be good replacements for plants in flower.

Calm days that are warm, but not too hot, are ideal for planting; if it's too windy, the root balls can easily dry out. Plants raised indoors must be hardened off before they are planted out, so that they'll tolerate the harsher conditions outside.

Treat any container-grown plant you buy to a good shot of liquid fertiliser at the recommended strength before you put it in open ground. That'll give it a helping hand until it can get its own supplies from the soil through new roots. The compost in the container doesn't usually have enough nutrients in it.

18

You need to water thoroughly both before and after planting. Remove biodegradable pots made from peat or recycled materials carefully: that way the plants will grow on better. If any container-grown perennials

Right: *Environmentally friendly biodegradable pots made from recycled materials*

Below: *Sawdust marks the boundaries between the areas set aside for planting.*

have got densely matted root balls, you'll encourage new root growth by gently teasing the roots apart.

The plants should fit easily into the holes you've dug for them. Dig out the hole with a spade or trowel, spread out the plant roots and fill the soil in all round. If you firm down the soil and water it, the plant's fine hair roots will make contact with the soil and its water-supply system. Plants that aren't put in firmly enough may dry out, but make certain that they're all standing upright, and at the same depth in the soil as before.

Space the plants according to the amount of room they're going to need later on — it's common to underestimate just how much a plant can grow. Thinking out a planting scheme in detail takes a lot of work, but it will prevent disappointment later on. A good plan will help you to work out colours, heights, growing habits and the number of plants you're going to need. Even professional gardeners draw out their intended planting scheme on the prepared bed, using a rake, a taut string or (even simpler) a scattering of sand. Try to think of unusual planting ideas yourself. There are so many ways to produce unexpected effects: you could plant bands of flowers, gently curving islands in the middle of the lawn, or diagonal stripes — or you could scatter seeds of poppy, *Lavatera trimestris*, dill (*Anethum graveolens*), grasses or cottage garden flowers.

19

Care and general maintenance

Every garden needs a bit of looking after, but it becomes a much more enjoyable job if you can limit it to the essentials. It's largely a matter of planning to avoid trouble and then tackling the few jobs that you *do* have to do in plenty of time.

Supporting weak shoots

Most plants manage quite well without any support, but sometimes it's advisable to make sure that plants can stand up to rain or wind, particularly if they're widely spaced or unusually tall (and therefore, perhaps, not entirely appropriate to the site). Whatever you do should be inconspicuous, but effective.

The most elegant solution is to use thin twigs or pea-sticks, bending over their tops among the groups of plants as soon as they start into growth. The shoots will work their way up the supports, eventually concealing them completely. If you don't have any twigs, you can resort to green-dyed bamboo canes: place them around and among the plants, and weave a cat's cradle of strings between them so that emerging shoots will grow through it. Alternatively, buy green-coated wire ties and stakes. You can adjust these to suit. This is all the more important as the supporting structure mustn't spoil the

appearance of the plant. You don't want clumps of perennials wrapped round with string!

Trimming and cutting back

A tour of the garden every week during the summer is all you need to take off damaged leaves or twigs that have finished flowering. Use a sharp knife or secateurs. This ensures that your flower garden always looks well cared for. It also ensures that further flowers will form from side-shoots, prolonging the flowering period.

Later on you'll hardly be able to see the twigs.

Delphinium, Leucanthemum vulgare, Erigeron, Maltese cross (*Lychnis chalcedonica*), purple loosestrife (*Lythrum salicaria*), candytuft (*Iberis*), *Nemesia strumosa* and water forget-me-not (*Myosotis palustris*) are just some of the perennials and annuals that you can cut back to a few inches above the ground straight after the first flush of flowers.

Soon more new shoots will form, ready for a second flowering in autumn.

Winter protection

In winter, grasses and picturesque seed-heads don't only provide food for the birds. They look even more attractive when they're glistening with frost or hooded in snow, and they bring life to the garden when everything else looks dead. So when you're doing the big autumn clean-up, leave suitable stems and stalks standing. Use shears or secateurs to cut the others down to just above ground level, composting or shredding the remains.

Shredded material from the autumn clear-up can be used as winter mulch for your more vulnerable perennials. The majority are hardy enough to survive most winters without any problem, as long as the frost isn't prolonged and doesn't penetrate too deeply into the

*Nothing for slugs here! Sweet alyssum (*Lobularia maritima*) remains unmolested.*

soil. A covering of bracken or straw is usually enough to protect the crowns of more tender varieties. Planting against a warm, south-facing wall will also give a lot of protection.

During mild spells some plants (e.g. *Eremurus*) come into premature growth and need a mulch or cloches to protect them from later frosts.

Slugs also benefit from mulches, and cause more winter losses than the cold weather. Try to reduce the population beforehand, and put down slug bait under the mulch.

Try not to walk on the borders during the winter, since wet soil will become compacted. This will leave it permanently wet and short of oxygen — a situation that can spell death to many plants. Use boards to walk on if you need to get to a plant.

Mulching

Cover the ground summer and winter with a 4-in (10-cm) deep layer of chopped straw or grass cuttings. This mulch layer keeps the soil loose and open, suppresses evaporation (which helps to save water), suppresses weed growth for a prolonged period, and serves as a welcome source of food for the many creatures that create humus — small animals, fungi and microbes.

Pests

Unfortunately, even a flower garden isn't immune to pests. If you attend to it every week, you're bound to notice where diseases or pests are trying to get a hold in good time. You can often keep an attack under control simply by removing affected plant material promptly.

In any case, it's difficult to deal with diseases in the garden. It's far better to use preventative measures. Build up the plants' strength by planting them well apart, by choosing disease-resistant varieties that suit the soil, and by well-judged applications of fertiliser.

If you're having problems with insects, a simple measure is to pull off or collect them as soon as they appear. With aphids, you can solve the problem by turning a powerful jet of water on them — although this can harm the plant. Otherwise you can spray them with a solution

of soft soap as a mild but effective domestic remedy: dissolve 5 oz of soap in a gallon of hot water (300 g in 10 litres).

It's even better to establish corners for beneficial insects in the garden. Here flowers rich in pollen can encourage hoverflies, green lacewings, parasitic wasps and soldier beetles. They and their offspring keep down pests such as aphids, whitefly, scale insects and red spider mite so effectively that you'll hardly need to take more radical measures.

Slugs and snails are among the biggest plagues in the flower garden. As soon as winter's over, they creep out from cracks in the ground, and from holes and hiding-places, or slip out from their overwintered eggs and attack the tender leaves of *Delphinium*, *Ligularia* and perennial sunflowers. Like the French and African marigold (*Tagetes*), these seem to be some of their favourite foods. A quick session with the pronged cultivator in spring should turn up any hidden gastropod eggs; if your particular corner of the natural world is in good order, and if there are enough hedgehogs, birds and ground beetles to tackle your slugs and snails, then the damage will be kept within bounds.

One way to keep slugs and snails under control is to go out in the dark with a torch and round them up while they're hard at work. Move them somewhere else, or kill them in a bucket of water with a little washing-up liquid added to it.

21

The scented garden in spring

Scented plants give the garden an extra dimension. If a rose has no fragrance, you're bound to be a little disappointed — and that same final, vital touch is missing from any romantic garden that has no scented plants.

In spring, competition among the scented plants for bees, bumble-bees, moths and butterflies is at its keenest. Vigorous contenders include violets, hyacinths, tulips, sweet rocket (*Hesperis matronalis*), wallflower (*Erysimum cheiri*), pansy and lily of the valley (*Convallaria majalis)*, to name but a few — and scent is only one of their weapons. There's also a range of scented flowering shrubs, such as viburnum, mock orange (*Philadelphus*) and wild hedge roses. All produce generous amounts of fragrance, and not just when the lilac blooms in May.

In a mild winter, the delicate pink flower clusters of scented viburnum (*Viburnum farreri*) open from December onwards. At winter's end, they are joined by violets and primroses (*Primula vulgaris*), quickly followed by cowslip (*Primula veris*), pansy, honesty (*Lunaria annua*) and alyssum. Towards the beginning of May the Siberian wallflower (*Erysimum allionii*) and its close relatives start to appear.

Many vigorous spring-flowering plants have colours that match those of scented flowers, and look good in bowls, window boxes, beds and borders. You can combine them with double daisy (*Bellis perennis*), forget-me-not (*Myosotis*), and the brightly coloured flowering bulbs.

The scent of irises is rather more restrained; by comparison white peonies are the heavy artillery. In China's imperial gardens magnificent flowering perennials were bred for thousands of years: now they compete with the first roses as they open at the end of May. Among carnations, the wild superb pink (*Dianthus superbus*), a native of the Alps with five elegantly feathered flower petals, produces the strongest scent.

Those pinks! It's hard to imagine them without scent, yet some cultivars have no fragrance, particularly among the summer-flowering varieties of the Indian pinks (*D. chinensis*). In the last century,there was a real collectors' craze for the scented ones; Cheddar pinks (*D. gratianopolitanus*), the traditional cottage-garden pinks (*D. plumarius*), carnations, sweet Williams (*D. barbatus*) — everyone wanted to have the most unusual variety.

Pinks go particularly well in places where you often stop and linger: near seats, in rock gardens, as edgings to gateways and paths, and in front gardens. They

Above: *Iris and stocks*

Left: *Sweet rocket (or dame's violet), peonies, pinks, Siberian wallflower, yarrow and roses provide a wealth of fragrance.*

will fit comfortably in window boxes and larger tubs.

Most pinks are short-lived perennials that need to be propagated regularly. Sweet William is raised as a biennial, sown between July and August. However, it always scatters so much seed that you don't have to worry about raising plants for the next year.

In early summer sweet Williams and roses complement each other, forming a romantic mixture of colours and fragrances that can hardly be bettered. If you want to, you can use blue lavender to add yet another aromatic element.

There's a choice among the sharper fragrances too: marigold (*Calendula*), oregano, rosemary, valerian, sage (*Salvia officinalis*), thyme, clary (*Salvia sclarea*) and — not to be despised as flowering perennials — chives (*Allium schoenoprasum*). These herbs needn't be confined to the box-hedged herb garden. As ornamentals in wild gardens, herbaceous borders, rock gardens or tubs, their attractive flowers and delicate, often grey-green, foliage make them successful partners to grasses, summer flowers or flowering perennials.

23

The scented garden in summer

Pavilions and summer-houses are at their most romantic when they're effectively a part of their surroundings, tightly wreathed in climbing plants such as pale blue wisteria (*Wisteria sinensis*), sweet smelling honeysuckle (*Lonicera caprifolium*), climbing roses or quick-growing nasturtium (*Tropaeolum majus*). When you're planning your garden, don't limit your thinking to colour and visual interest; remember to consider the fragrances, too.

If there isn't much room near your favourite seat, then vanilla-scented heliotrope (*Heliotropium arborescens*), ornamental tobacco (*Nicotiana*), petunias, yellow evening primroses (*Oenothera*) or the four o'clock flower (*Mirabilis*), with its fragrance of oranges, can all find a home in pots, terracotta containers and flower boxes.

Among the low growing mound- or mat-forming summer flowers, sweet alyssum (*Lobularia maritima*) makes a good, strong impression, with a pleasant honey fragrance that is particularly strong in the evening. There are white, pink and

Scented roses and Dianthus plumarius *complement one another superbly.*

dark-pink flowered varieties; it self-seeds readily, and it's perfect for those rather forlorn spots between stones and on dry walls. Ugly cement blocks will effectively disappear when loose mounds of *Lobularia maritima* spill out from all the cracks. Flowering continues through until November.

Nasturtium, too, is long-lasting. There are varieties with a bushy habit such as 'Whirlybird' and the Jewel series, as well as the climbing form, which snakes its way carelessly round stones and walls and climbs high on tree-trunks, trellises and rose arches.

Sweet peas (*Lathyrus odoratus*) also like to make their way to the light. There are bushy-growing varieties, but the better-known climbers will quickly make their way to the top of fences, trellises and brushwood. The more flowers you cut, the more abundantly they'll set new ones. Arranged in bunches, they fill rooms with their delicate perfume, just like mignonette (*Reseda odorata*), an insignificant-looking annual that gives off an elusive but very sweet scent, particularly in the evenings.

Seed for these annuals will only cost a few pence. They grow quickly and flourish almost everywhere.

Once summer has passed its peak, there's a shortage of scented perennials, but there's a lot more nectar on offer, and butterflies, in particular, will be drawn to it. Numerous clumps of phlox will make up for the shortage, and in the evenings

the yellow flower funnels of *Oenothera biennis* and the pale pink inflorescences of the soapwort (*Saponaria*) give off streams of gentle perfume. All three are large, striking border perennials which also make good cut flowers.

Herbs are increasingly found outside the area reserved for culinary and medicinal plants, as part of the perennial border. Many are ornamental in themselves, notably thyme, the pale yellow rue (*Ruta graveolens*), red bergamot (*Monarda didyma*), hyssop (*Hyssopus*

officinalis), in dark blue and pink varieties and the brownish-white oregano.

> Try the silvery white ornamental forms of *Salvia officinalis*, wormwood (*Artemisia absinthium*), mugwort (*A. vulgaris*) and southernwood (*A. abrotanum*) as a complement roses, shrubs and delphiniums, as a spicy-scented ground cover, or planted beneath standard or tub-grown plants.

Scented flowers that can be raised from seed

Botanical name	Common name	Flowering months	Height in in (cm)
Agastache mexicana	Mexican giant hyssop	Jul.–Sep.	48 (120)
Anthemis tinctoria	ox-eye chamomile	Jun.–Jul.	24 (60)
Asperula orientalis	woodruff	Jun.–Jul.	16 (40)
Calendula officinalis	marigold	Jun.–Oct.	16 (40)
Centaurea moschata	sweet sultan	Jul.	20 (50)
Chenopodium botrys	Jerusalem oak	Jul.	40 (100)
Clarkia elegans	clarkia	Jul.	20 (50)
Dracocephalum moldavicum		Jul.–Sep.	24 (60)
Erysimum allionii	Siberian wallflower	Jun.–Aug.	16 (40)
Erysimum cheiri	wallflower	Apr.–Jun.	20 (50)
Iberis amara	candytuft	Jun.–Jul.	12 (30)
Hesperis matronalis	sweet rocket/dame's violet	Apr.–May	24 (60)
Hyssopus officinalis	hyssop	Aug.–Oct.	16 (40)
Lathyrus odoratus	sweet pea	Jun.–Aug.	48 (120)
Lobularia maritima	sweet alyssum	May–Nov.	8 (20)
Lunaria annua	honesty	Apr.–May	32 (80)
Matthiola bicornis	night-scented stock	Jun.–Jul.	12 (30)
Matthiola incana	Brompton stock	Jun.–Aug.	16 (40)
Mentzelia lindleyi	blazing star	Jun.–Jul.	16 (40)
Ocimum basilicum anisum	aniseed basil	Jul.–Aug.	12 (30)
Ocimum basilicum cinnamomum	cinnamon basil	Jul.–Aug.	12 (30)
Oenothera biennis	evening primrose	Jul.–Sep.	28 (70)
Reseda odorata	mignonette	Jun.–Aug.	12 (30)
Salpiglossis sinuata	velvet trumpet flower	Jun.–Sep.	24 (60)
Salvia sclarea	clary	Jun.–Aug.	40 (100)
Scabiosa atropurpurea	sweet scabious	Jun.–Aug.	24 (60)
Tagetes tenuifolia	striped Mexican marigold	Jun.–Oct.	12 (30)
Tropaeolum majus	nasturtium	Jun.–Oct.	12–60 (30–150)

Wild gardens for the birds and the bees

What is a wild garden? An area of natural wilderness, where visitors sneak in to catch a glimpse of the idyll? A paradise with a garden pond and a sunny bank? Or a patch of cottage garden where red poppies, foxgloves, sunflowers and native honeysuckle can grow almost unchecked?

An area like this doesn't have to cover more than a few square yards/metres. It can be a corner full of beneficial plants bought as a mixture of annual seeds, or an area designed with the ecology in mind, including, for instance, plants for feeding bees (buckwheat works wonders!), bird baths, dry-stone walls, and piles of dead wood or wood stacks where beneficial creatures like hedgehogs, ground beetles, ladybirds and green lacewings can find shelter for the winter.

Seed merchants and garden centres offer a wide range of wild flower seeds you can raise yourself, as well as ready-grown native plants. Cowslip (*Primula veris*), anemone, meadow sage (*Salvia pratensis*), cuckoo flower (*Cardamine pratensis*), cranes-bill (*Geranium*), columbine (*Aquilegia*), mullein (*Verbascum densiflorum*), carline thistle (*Carlina vulgaris*) or — for the wet area — elecampane (*Inula helenium*), yellow flag (*Iris pseudacorus*), yellow loosestrife (*Lysimachia punctata*), *Lythrum salicaria* and hemp agrimony (*Eupatorium cannabinum*) are just some examples of native plants that will bear comparison with flowering perennials from anywhere in the world.

Native trees and shrubs form the framework for a wild planting scheme, offering food and accommodation for a large number of insects and small animals. The top place in the ecological value charts goes to the oak (*Quercus*), which supports more than 50 species including butterflies, beetles, bugs, sawflies and aphids. The number-two spot is taken by the pussy willow, followed by hawthorn, sloe, hazel, wild rose and rowan.

Meadow corners are suitable for a wild garden, and so are open planting schemes on sandy, stony or boggy ground. Here you can plant your native perennials according to taste

(and according to the company that you want them to keep). Wild vegetation will soon take up residence between them; you can exercise a degree of control with *Leucanthemum vulgare* or feverfew (*Tanacetum parthenium*), and by sowing annual or biennial flowers.

We strongly recommend the red field poppy (*Papaver rhoeas*); in summer, it transforms the garden into an impressionist-like sea of colour. Yellow corn marigold (*Chrysanthemum segetum*), wild blue cornflowers

Above: *An ecological corner with low-growing wild flowers*

Left: *A wild garden can look as beautiful as this.*

(*Centaurea cyanus*), pink corn cockle (*Agrostemma githago*), white camomile (*Matricaria recutita*), blue field larkspur (*Delphinium consolida*) and red pheasant's eye (*Adonis autumnalis*) are wild flowers from the flora at the edge of fields, but they'll also create bright spots of colour in the wild garden. In any case, it's worth trying out seed mixtures of this type — they're always worth the money, and they don't need much looking after. And if you're willing to make the experiment, you may make a pleasant discovery among the less familiar wild flowers.

Sow your seeds broadcast in suitably sunny places (e.g. in front of or behind the fence) and rake them in level. They'll soon start shooting up. From the end of May till the frost, new colours will keep appearing, and with them a fresh supply of nectar and pollen — just what butterflies, bees, bumble bees, hoverflies, green lacewings and soldier beetles are waiting for.

In their larval forms, most of these insects eagerly devour aphids. They also like scale insects, whiteflies and mites.

 A wild garden is home to many beneficial insects. As well as being ecologically interesting, this also cuts down on maintenance.

Cottage gardens

The origins of cottage gardens are lost in the depths of time. At first they were little more than yards for animals, but gradually small enclosures were used to bring together useful herbs gathered from the surrounding area. Vegetables and (eventually) flowers were introduced.

Traditionally, plants would be jumbled together in a riot of colour, with no thought for design. Many annuals were left to self-sow freely, adding to the general profusion. Vegetables were sometimes allowed to mingle with flowers. Herbs, too, were mixed in, adding colour and scent to the scene — though the ones that were used most often would be planted near the kitchen door for easy access.

The plants had to be tough to cope with the competition in the crowded borders, and to fight off pests and diseases we can now control. They were also easy to propagate: busy cottagers had little time for fussy plants. Hardly surprising, then, that so many of the old-fashioned flowers have come down to us.

Paths of gravel, natural stone, and clinker or a simple scattering scattering of softwood chippings divide and link the beds. In them grow vegetables, herbs and low-maintenance flowers. Despite the apparent disorder, everything has

found its appropriate setting: many plants have seeded themselves in congenial places. But plants can't thrive for long where conditions of light or moisture aren't right for them. This is

particularly true of the tasty, fine-limbed dill, and of *Calendula officinalis, Chrysanthemum leucanthemum*, poppies, cosmea (*Cosmos bipinnatus*), *Myosotis* and *Tropaeolum majus*.

The garden used to be the housewife's domain. As well as vegetables sufficient for the family (almost invariably a large

Neat box hedges enclose a riot of floral colour.

one), flowers were and still are very popular with country people. And novelties are not taboo — quite the opposite. If something proves its worth, it's used in exchange and recommended to other people. For example, *Lavatera trimestris* 'Silver Cup' (pink) and 'Mont Blanc' (white) are relatively new strains, but their rich display of flowers has won them admittance to cottage gardens as a matter of course.

Rose arches give sky-blue morning glory (*Ipomoea tricolor*) and climbing *Tropaeolum* the chance to wind their way upwards. *Clematis* are old cottage favourites for covering arches. Among the most popular is the exuberant *C. montana*, which is hardy and needs virtually no maintenance.

Typical annuals with a long tradition are marigold (*Calendula officinalis*), love-in-a-mist (*Nigella damascena*), cornflower (*Centaurea cyanus*), larkspur (*Delphinium consolida*), Shirley poppy, sweet William (*Dianthus barbatus*), horned violet (*Viola cornuta*), love-lies-bleeding (*Amaranthus caudatus*), Chinese aster (*Callistephus chinensis*), snapdragon (*Antirrhinum majus*), *Godetia grandiflora*, balsam (*Impatiens balsamina*), clarkias and zinnias.

Some flowers have a simplicity that has endeared them to generations of cottage gardeners. For example, the common lawn daisy (*Bellis perennis*) has produced several strains of double flowers, as well as pink

Feverfew (Tanacetum parthenium), marigolds (Calendula officinalis), mullein (Verbascum densiflorum), California poppy (Eschscholzia californica) and lilies

and red-coloured blooms. These have been used not only as bedding but also for lining the edges of paths and borders.

Chrysanthemum carinatum produces marvellous beds, rich in colour; they can be almost meadow-like in character, though the flowers are also suitable for cutting.

The baby blue-eyes (*Nemophila menziesii*) from Australia is another flower that you must sow broadcast in patches. Its little blue, bell-like flowers make a glorious scented carpet. Perennials such as the age-old Maltese

cross (*Lychnis chalcedonica*) offer a clear contrast to this. Its brilliant red inflorescences provide points of strong emphasis, along with white *Leucanthemum × superbum* and deep-blue delphiniums. Baby's breath (*Gypsophila*) or the pale-green lady's mantle (*Alchemilla mollis*) give a group of perennials a touch of delicate haziness.

Golden yellow *Lysimachia congestiflora*, hollyhocks (*Alcea rosea*), phlox, bergamot (*Monarda didyma*) and sweet-smelling lilies are robust summer flowers. Spring is unthinkable without bleeding heart (*Dicentra spectabilis*); this looks good in the company of bright bluebells (*Hyacinthoides non-scriptus*) and pastel-shaded *Aquilegia*.

The flaming-red oriental poppy (*Papaver orientale*) contrasts with white *Leucanthemum × superbum* and blue delphiniums. All three yield good flowers for cutting too. Fragrant cottage-garden flowers include burning bush (*Dictamnus albus*), *Dianthus gratianopolitanus* and above all the peonies.

And you can't have a cottage garden without roses, whether they're shrubs and climbers. Old garden roses and the robust English roses, with varieties such as 'Constance Spry' (pink), 'Graham Thomas' (golden-yellow), 'Abraham Derby' (pink and gold) and 'Winchester Cathedral' (white) combine the best of the old characteristics with the finest achievements of modern breeding — beautiful, fully double flowers.

Formal gardens and carpet bedding

Over the centuries our gardens have seen many changes in the name of fashion, especially fashions introduced from the continent. Sometimes we have preferred formal gardens, where line, pattern and proportion are all-important; at other times a 'natural' informality has been the order of the day. In the past, gardening was often carried out on a vast scale, embracing entire estates; but even then, many ideas would filter down to smaller gardens.

In the Victorian period bedding became all the rage. It could be seen in the most elaborate of formal designs, in private gardens as well as in municipal parks. Enthusiasm for this style of gardening is still with us a hundred years later, despite a reaction against it at the beginning of this century.

When you're looking at the few square yards/metres of a town garden, then 'small is beautiful'. Terracotta containers or tasteful ceramics can create a southern ambience. You could have rustic stone paving, or elegant natural stone. You can install tub-grown plants, raised beds, small pruned trees and fragrant box hedges. Not everyone can work up an enthusiasm for wild, rampant vegetation, but if you want it, you can combine it very well with the

formal style. Simply divide your garden into 'rooms'; that way you can have a formal 'front parlour' and arrange the rest to be low-maintenance and close to nature.

Between walls and hedges, where space is short, you'll often have to limit the growth of your plants, so if you're breeding annual bedding plants you'll need to aim for a compact habit. Plants such as begonias, floss flower (*Ageratum*), sweet alyssum (*Lobularia maritima*), zonal pelargoniums, petunias, *Tagetes* or dahlias can display their beauties much more effectively in a confined area.

The formal bed depends for its style on geometry: on circles, rectangles, squares, and low hedges of box, *Santolina*,

lavender, rosemary or other fragrant herbs. The dark or white-felted green makes an elegant frame for the brilliance of the summer flowers, which can now be planted in a jumble of colour, just as the fancy happens to take you.

It's true you'll have to cut these low hedges once or twice a year, but you'll save all the work involved in measuring out, staking and planning.

Annual summer flowers such as *Senecio maritima* 'Silver-dust', silver feather (*Pyrethrum ptarmicaeflorum*) or the white-and-yellow dwarf marguerites (*Chrysanthemum paludosum*)

Artistic carpet bedding has lost none of its appeal.

A round bed of mixed tulips, planted with pansies

are also good for 'framed' planting. Other very suitable plants are lobelia (use white and blue alternately), *Begonia semperflorens* in red, pink or white, dwarf asters or low-growing snapdragon in clear colours.

In spring, white, pink or red *Bellis perennis*, blue *Myosotis*, pansies and wallflowers can form bold and fragrant carpets of flowers. You can also use them to make curved bands of flowers; as they weave across the lawn they will give your whole design a cheery lift. Flowering bulbs such as hyacinths, narcissi or tulips vary the theme.

In summer all bedding plants are permissible, in pleasant and ornamental arrangements. On the outside put low-growing plants such as sweet alyssum in

If you have a surplus of tulip bulbs from earlier planting schemes, plan a multi-coloured bed. Plant a thoroughgoing mixture in a circular frame, and let them bloom as they come — early and late varieties, tall and short. Plant white or yellow pansies underneath to unify the whole and to make this vibrant display stand out in your garden.

white or pink, *Begonia semperflorens*, *Chrysanthemum paludosum* or *Ageratum*.

For somewhat taller bushes, try *Nicotiana alata*, *Pelargonium*, scarlet sage (*Salvia splendens*), farinaceous sage (*S. farinacea*), flame nettle (*Coleus*),

Heliotropium arborescens, *Tagetes* or chamomile (*Chamaemelum nobile*).

One or more container-grown plants in each bed provide an artistic focus and a 'third storey'; use plants such as palms, flowering banana (*Musa ornata*), dragon tree (*Dracaena draco*), *Agave* or standard forms of *Fuchsia*, *Argyranthemum frutescens* or *Lantana*. Flowers at eye level are always an attraction where plants will be seen at close quarters, but they have other uses too. Plants with leaves that are green-and-white striped or brownish-red can be very effective.

31

Climbers — the third dimension

Plants that are struggling upward or tumbling downward invariably draw our attention. Climbing plants can give an appearance of breadth to small and narrow gardens, walls and wooden frontages, and this kind of garden also seems to look comfortable and welcoming. When everything's in full bloom, the result can be a miniature paradise.

Walls, fences, rose arches, mesh sight-screens, walls for climbers, trellises, wires and strings: all these things give plants something to hold on to as they creep, twine, or climb towards the light. They're also ideal for shaping the space; they divide and separate, perhaps screening off a garden or patio and so opening up some new and interesting perspectives. They may block the line of sight entirely or — as in the case of a pergola — create a light and decorative element. Either way, they can provide the perfect backdrop for a show of flowers, especially flowers with delicate nuances of colour. Tall perennials such as delphinium, iris, golden rod (*Solidago*), ox-eye (*Buphthalmum*), coneflower (*Rudbeckia*), *Eryngium*, pampas grass (*Cortaderia selloana*) or *Eupatorium* can also look really striking against a background of climbing plants.

The trunks of many fruit trees, ornamental trees and larger bushes (e.g. lilac) benefit from a little colour. Plant annual climbers such as climbing nasturtium (*Tropaeolum majus*), Black-eyed Susan (*Thunbergia alata*), morning glory (*Ipomoea tricolor*), or the golden-yellow canary creeper (*Tropaeolum peregrinum*), which will also flower in shade.

There's a whole range of tried-and-tested shrubs and bushes which can easily lighten the atmosphere in your garden. Your choice isn't limited. Climbing roses and clematis, honeysuckle (*Lonicera periclymenum*), Chinese wisteria (*Wisteria sinensis*) and Virginia creeper (*Parthenocissus*), all have beautiful blossoms and leaves; if you want food, too, consider grapevine (*Vitis*), blackberry (*Rubus fruticosus*) and hop (*Humulus*).

You'll find some very fast-growing plants among the annuals. Gourds (e.g. the bottle-gourds) can quickly produce shoots up to 16 ft (5 m) long. Their fruits can look very exotic.

*Everlasting pea (*Lathyrus latifolius*) in full bloom*

They can also grow up to 7 ft (2 m) long, and come in useful for handicrafts. Botanically speaking, they're species of the *Cucurbita* and *Lagenaria*. Scarlet runner beans (*Phaseolus coccineus*) look splendid with their brilliant red or pink flowers, and they're also very useful in the kitchen, producing long, tasty pods and big pink and black-flecked seeds. They tolerate a windy site and you can grow them very cheaply from seed — all in all a bargain way to cover summer-houses, sheds, fences and patios with foliage.

Ipomoea quamoclit, with its sumptuous brilliant red and yellow flowers, flourishes in larger tubs or on supports up to 7 ft (2 m) high, as does the

 It's fun to collect beautiful climbers, but space can often become a problem. One solution is to use beanpoles stuck upright in the ground, or else to train your plants onto coarse-fibred coir ropes dangling from a pergola.This can create a surprisingly natural look. A tent for climbing plants (the kind of thing children use for covering with runner beans) can also be very decorative. Push a pole firmly into the ground and run strings to the plants all around it. Plant other kinds of climber, too — give your imagination a free hand!

Ipomoea quamoclit *comes from Brazil.*

purplish-lilac *Maurandia barclaiana*. In sunny spots this is also a way to grow the lilac-blue cup-and-saucer vine (*Cobaea scandens*) and the exotic Chilean glory flower (*Eccremocarpus scaber*), with its little yellow and orange-red flowers. There's a interesting choice of flowering climbers already available, and new varieties continue to widen their scope.

Perennials in containers

How do you decide whether a plant is a summer flower, a perennial or a houseplant? If it's January, and you've just bought a potted *Campanula carpatica* in full bloom, it's pretty hard to classify. After all, this so-called houseplant used to be an open-air perennial that flowered in high summer.

All year round in nurseries and garden centres you'll find plants for bowls and pots constantly in flower. More and more perennials are being forced, as nurserymen control temperature or day-length to make them bloom by appointment. And many of these new ways to use plants are very interesting; they open up entirely new ideas for the window box, the patio, or even the conservatory.

So cast your eye over a small selection of the frost-hardy plants. They're far too good just to throw away. Whether they're in bowls or tubs, window boxes or hanging baskets (though ideally in a permanent position) they can continue to grow, providing both a lively display and a low-maintenance addition to your patio flowers, conifers, small shrubs and bushes.

In autumn, there are plenty of *Aster dumosus* available in pots.

Take the opportunity to search out good varieties — the ones that offer resistance to mildew, as well as a low-growing habit and the promise of interesting colours. Potted asters in flower will attract hordes of insects. You can plant them comfortably in bowls, integrate them into permanent planting schemes, or incorporate them into the garden later on.

Bellflowers (*Campanula*) flower from June until August. Two of the low-growing species, reaching 6–8 in (15–20 cm) in height, are particularly popular: *C. carpatica*, with its

Something a little different — perennials in bowls

large, pale-blue or white saucer flowers and its slightly hairy leaves, and *C. portenschlagiana*, which can offer smaller, more intensely blue flowers. Planted out in the rock garden, they'll add lustre to the scene for many years.

Dicentra spectabilis comes in pink and in white varieties, but they're only really attractive in spring. They look good in terracotta containers and beautiful bowls, but the leaves and the delicate inflorescences soon disappear. Even so, it would be a mistake to throw the plant away at this point. It's better to put a summer-flowering plant next to it in the container — *Impatiens walleriana* or *Viola cornuta* perhaps — and let nature take its course until the next spring.

Irises go well with evergreen shrubs and trees, particularly when the container is placed in a hot, sunny spot. Sadly, their spectacular blooms don't last long. Petunias, Livingstone daisies (*Dorotheanthus bellidiformis*), *Santolina*, pelargoniums or pot roses are follow-on plants that bloom over a longer period. *Iris sibirica*, the blue Siberian flag, goes well with water or in semi-shaded parts of patios, and with hydrangeas or ornamental grasses.

The scabious (*Scabiosa*) is a hedgerow and meadow plant, and flowers in summer from June to October. The little pale-blue flower-heads aren't particularly conspicuous, but they attract butterflies of many

*Bleeding heart (*Dicentra spectabilis*) is a flower of charm and beauty.*

species like a magnet, even when they're planted high in a window box. Nurseries specialising in perennials know this, and offer the plants for sale in full bloom.

The same applies to the larger stonecrops (*Sedum*). These robust, untemperamental members of the Crassulaceae are suitable for sun and partial shade. In late autumn, the light or dark pink inflorescences burst into flower, and roof gardens or patios wake once more in a blaze of glory. It's really quite amazing what a crowd of butterflies, bees and bumble-bees will gather round these plants for the pleasure of topping up their nectar supply

It's not essential to have all containers in full sun; plenty of plants will enjoy lightly shaded conditions, perhaps against the north-facing wall of a house. Ferns and hostas are two attractive groups of plants that thrive in shade, especially if you keep the compost moist.

The beautiful blue-flowering *Liriope muscari* is another versatile plant. With its grass-like leaves and round flowers, it looks rather like a grape hyacinth. You can put it on display on the patio in a terracotta pot, or keep it in flower through the height of summer and into the autumn in a damp, cool conservatory or bathroom.

The white-green gardener's garters (*Phalaris arundinacea* 'Picta') is a pretty, completely robust ornamental grass, which shouldn't disappoint you even under difficult conditions of sun or shade. The lively colour of its leaves makes dark areas of plants look interesting, even in the rain. In the garden you need to be a little careful: in over-congenial surroundings this beautiful grass will spread uncontrollably, but in a tub it's very decorative.

Flowers all around the pond

Where the ground is moist, and marshland merges with the water's edge, vegetation can grow particularly lush. Plants that can survive in these conditions are generally very robust and adaptable. Even so, the 'wick effect' of the soil around a pond isn't always desirable. Since the pond liner will prevent moisture from entering the soil, you'll need to make special provision for growing moisture-loving plants around the edge. You could take the top of the liner further out and fill the resulting ledge with soil, or you could deliberately allow the pond to overflow in certain places.

To match the character of the pond you need a loose, informal planting scheme. As far as possible, it should provide attractive flowers and forms throughout the garden year. The low-growing, clump-forming habit of blue lungwort (*Pulmonaria officinalis*), or of *Bergenia*, with its decorative shining leaves and pink flowers in spring, makes an effective contrast to 'islands' of high-towering *Iris sibirica*, grasses or daylilies (*Hemerocallis*).

It's important to have ground-cover plants that will disguise the edge of the pond with their leaves and tendrils. The Siberian bugloss (*Brunnera macrophylla*) has a long flowering season in April and May and is happy in the shady areas. Alternatives include *Tiarella cordifolia*, *Omphalodes verna* (similar to the forget-me-not) and *Waldsteinia ternata*, which has yellow flowers. Another very adaptable plant is creeping Jenny (*Lysimachia nummularia*), which is covered in yellow blooms in the summer and takes up residence virtually all round the pond.

Astilbe in shades of red, pink and white, blazing star (*Liatris spicata*), purple loosestrife (*Lythrum salicaria*) and yellow loosestrife (*Lysimachia punctata*) all adorn the pond edge with strong colours in high summer. And throughout the autumn, coneflower (*Rudbeckia*) and pink *Eupatorium cannabinum* attract hundreds of butterflies.

Other, special plants can draw the eye in prominent positions between these focal points — clumps of plantain lily (*Hosta*), for instance, with their wonderful blue-green or white-green leaves, or the cream or pink inflorescences of *Rodgersia*. For autumn we particularly recommend the turtle-head (*Chelone obliqua*) with its strangely shaped pink flowers, which last well when they're cut.

Glittering, cooling water gives every garden something fresh and natural. Dragonflies, frogs and toads settle alongside the stream, and birds come to bathe. In short, the layout of a garden pond nearly always calls for a wild garden around it.

A glorious display of annuals on the pond bank is a fairly inexpensive pleasure.

You get a wonderful combination of colours — purple and yellow — if you plant *Lythrum salicaria* and *Coreopsis verticillata* next to each other in small groups. Both of them flower at the same time.

Illuminated fountains with circular or angular basins fit easily into a planting scheme of formal or well-filled beds planted with colourful annuals. An exotic-looking bed full of magnificently coloured waterlilies (*Nymphaea*) is set off beautifully by a carpet of flowers — *Lobularia maritima, Nicotiana alata* and *Heliotropium arborescens* — with Indian shot (*Canna indica*) and tall *Ricinus* planted between the two areas.

You'll need a sensitive touch if you want to make plants such as *Zinnia, Tagetes, Salvia splendens* and *Ageratum* blend seamlessly into the pond landscape. The compact, bushy habit of some varieties of these plants doesn't really go with the loose or delicate habit of the plants that grow in or beside the pond.

By contrast, flowers that share the characteristics of wild flowers blend in well. Even a meadow-like planting scheme can become a prize exhibit, with annual or perennial ornamental grasses creating a link to shrubs and trees and decorative elements.

You've got to be careful with brilliant, pure colours. Summer flowers work well on the pond bank if you use shades of blue tending towards red (as in *Lobelia* 'Fan Cinnabar Rose'), or warm shades of ochre, rather than pure yellow (as with the striped Mexican marigold, *Tagetes tenuifolia* 'Lulu'), and replace the cold white of a rain daisy (*Osteospermum prostratum*) with the white tones of *Chrysanthemum paludosum*, broken by yellow stamens.

You can also sow flower-seed broadcast between the clumps of perennials, or on open beds. Blue woodruff (*Galium odoratum*), *Nemophila menziesii* and, in spring, *Myosotis* all spread to cover the ground.

Larkspur (*Delphinium solida*), *Lavatera trimestris* 'Silver Cup' (pink) and Shirley poppies (*Papaver rhoeas* Shirley series) all have a light, loose habit. *Cosmos bipinnatus* fits in very well. From July onwards, there's plenty of colourful activity, with crowds of butterflies and bees taking their fill of nectar.

 It doesn't take a lot of money, or a lot of work, to sow one of the species-rich wild-flower mixtures broadcast along the edge of a pond. You can also use it to fill up any gaps. It will produce a constantly changing display of flowers from May through to October — and insects, including many beneficial ones, will find it a real treasure trove.

Colourful rock gardens

Most rock garden flowers bloom between April to June. As they do in their mountain homelands, plants like aubrietias (*Aubrieta*), yellow *Alyssum saxatile*, white or pink *Arabis caucasica,* and dwarf phlox produce brilliant and competing colours to attract insects. The spring vegetation is often profuse, but the perennial flowers that follow are rather less exuberant. If you want a miniature flower landscape in the summer, as well, you'll need considerable skill.

Mound-forming bellflowers such as *Campanula portenschlagiana* and *C. carpatica*, fragrant creeping thyme (*Thymus serpyllum*) and the various *Sedum* species do make good alternatives, but a bit of colour from summer flowers won't hurt. For instance, you can start using *Aster dumosus* in August.

Many of the smaller perennials have very clear, intense colours that give unmistakable signals to the first insects as they search for nourishment. You can keep these glorious colours going right through the summer; the intensely blue annual forget-me-not (*Myosotis*), white-and-yellow feverfew (*Tanacetum parthenium*), *Phlox drummondii* in all its colours, and dwarf zinnias perform all these functions.

If you've already planned your rock garden and its final shape is (literally) set in stone, you'll hardly want to change it now. But if you're looking for a finishing touch in small-scale terraced beds, larger troughs and stone niches, or a way of filling gaps in already existing planting schemes within the rock garden, why not plant some annual summer flowers?

Sun plants (*Portulaca grandiflora*) in one corner, with delicate, fragile-looking *Nemophila menziesii* next to and in front of them, create a picture of vulnerability; but the plants are in the right place, safe between stones. The poor man's orchid (*Schizanthus*) fits into another corner, its flowers shimmering in many different colours.

The next gap can be occupied by sweet William or *Godetia grandiflora*. Treasure flower (*Gazania*), *Arctotis* and the Swan River daisy (*Brachycome iberidifolia*) are all solitaries, ideal for the smaller gaps. The mesembryanthemum *Dorotheanthus bellidiformis* spreads itself out in the sun: try to put it somewhere where you'll have a good view of it.

Despite the great variety of plants in a relatively small space, this sort of juxtaposition of plants doesn't look as if it's been thrown together. All of them seem very retiring in company, and are only revealed in their full glory when you look at them more closely.

Delicate mixtures of low-growing flowers such as the Japanese flower lawn, or one of the wild-flower mixtures, don't demand much in the way of time or effort.

This rock garden goes on flowering all the time, even in summer.

Two cheerful annuals that resow themselves after the first planting are the delightful *Omphalodes linifolia*, with its white flowers and grey leaves, and the poached-egg flower (*Limnanthes douglasii*), named for the distinctively shaped yellow-and-white flowers that appear in May and June.

In a rock garden, dwarf peas (*Lathyrus vernus*) won't be overshadowed by sweet peas (*Lathyrus odoratus*). These attractive miniature editions grow 8-12 in (20-30 cm) tall, and flower in spring.

Dry gardens and scree beds

A dry garden is both attractive and labour-saving. Whether it's flat, like a shingle beach, or built on a steep slope like a Mediterranean hillside, its plants are robust, holding their own against the searing sun. Many of them exude the intense scent of the Mediterranean scrubland, the maquis, bringing back holiday memories. Silvery-white *Artemisia absinthium*, dark pink *Thymus serpyllum*, *Oregano vulgare*, *Santolina*, *Ruta graveolens* and *Hyssopus officinalis* — many of the decorative herbs are very comfortable in dry conditions. And then there are the lovely everlasting flowers from Europe, North America, and especially from Australia.

Straw flowers (*Helichrysum bracteatum*), paper flowers (*Xeranthemum annuum*), *Helipterum manglesii* and ornamental grasses are all top tips. For many months after they've really finished flowering, the dried flowers continue to provide a colourful display. As companion plants, think about uncomplicated desert dwellers like California poppy, thistles like the teasel (or fuller's thistle, *Dipsacus fullonum*), the magnificent steel-blue cardoon (*Cynara cardunculus*), alpine masters of survival like *Carlina*, or groundcover plants like the azure-blue Chilean bellflower (*Nolana paradoxa*).

Once you start to look at them more carefully, you will suddenly find that many well-known garden plants are nowhere near as sensitive as we like to think. For example, *Lavatera trimestris*, *Cosmos bipinnatus*, poppies,

Steps filled with flowers lead down to the garden pond.

Gypsophila or Cape gooseberry (*Physalis alkekengi*) grow particularly well on lean, free-draining soils, provided, of course, that the sun is shining — and the more, the better.

You'll often find gravel and stones being used to cover the ground around buildings, or to soften the appearance of a sunny patio. Many people try to establish grasses, lavender, *Yucca* and *Sedum* here as long-term plants. These cope very well with this extremely dry situation, as long as you play a hose over them every so often to give them the water they need.

A planting scheme of grasses and succulents can look rather bare. To prevent this happening, you could plant pure-blue pimpernel (*Anagallis* 'Blue Light') in front of them; this will form spreading mounds.

Sweet alyssum dotted loosely around creates a very delicate effect; despite its low-growing habit it looks good against the background of stones.

When you're doing a spring clean, you'll need to rake through the gravel and stones to get rid of all the dead leaves (and root out any weeds). But you should always try not to disturb the perennial plants, and do resow any annuals that you want to use.

Plenty of flowers, even in the shade

Gardens tend to become increasingly shaded. There's not much you can do to change that; often it's what you want.

Plants are supposed to grow quickly. We plant perennials, shrubs and trees so that a new arrangement will quickly become intimate and cosy: and we finish up with plants that are far too close together. After only two or three years, more and more shadows appear, and the plants start to grow more slowly, because shrubs and trees are monopolising the available light and air.

Experience suggests that gardens are at their most beautiful and varied two or three years after they've been laid out. If you want to keep a garden in full growth after that, you must avoid too many ornamental shrubs and evergreen trees and bushes, or thin them back so that there's nothing to obstruct morning or evening sunlight.

Shade also means less rain (because trees and shrubs shelter the perennials and annuals), fewer nutrients and far greater competition. Many beautiful plants are forced to give up and make way for others more able to cope with difficult conditions.

This doesn't mean a shaded planting scheme has to look dreary — quite the opposite! Rhododendron, azalea, sheep laurel (*Kalmia angustifolia*), and *Andromeda polifolia* are all trees and shrubs that bring colour into the garden. They also provide a frame for the perennials and annuals, allowing the garden to shine in all its glory when they flower.

Pelargoniums prove to be remarkably resilient, giving a virtuoso performance despite limited water and light. In damp, shady places, *Impatiens walleriana* can transform dark areas of the garden. Choose light colours if you want to make the garden look wider.

There are only a few annuals that will tolerate real shade. Examples include New Guinea impatiens, fibrous-rooted begonias (*Begonia semperflorens*), tuberous begonias (*B. × tuberhybrida*), honesty (*Lunaria annua*) and dame's violet (*Hesperis matronalis*). Semi-shaded situations, on the other hand, are no problem. You can plant flowering bulbs such as snowdrops (*Galanthus nivalis*), spring snowflakes (*Leucojum vernum*), *Scilla* and glory-of-the-snow (*Chionodoxa*), winter aconites (*Eranthis hyemalis*), bluebells and above all *Narcissus* and *Crocus*. Before the bushes and trees show the first tints of green, the bulbs find time to flower and to complete their development by maturing new bulbs.

Once they're well established, shade-loving perennials don't need much looking after — provided, of course, that they're on the right soil and in the right situation. This blanket of plants can manage with less moisture and fewer nutrients. To help the perennials hold their own in the thick mat of tree- and shrub-roots, apply a 4-in (10-cm) deep layer of compost, leaf-mould or bark compost before planting.

These materials, along with wood chippings to suppress weed growth, are available at a very reasonable price from most garden centres, and also from specialist suppliers dealing in forest products.

Enrich the humus layer still further with slow-release organic fertilisers, adding e.g. 1½ oz/sq yd (50 g/m^2) hoof-and-horn and 1¼ oz/sq yd (40 g/m^2) bonemeal. Later on the plants' leaves and roots will largely fend for themselves.

Main perennials for the summer

For north-facing sites, shaded areas near trees and shrubs, and areas close to the house, there are decorative perennials that combine an elegant appearance with a long flowering period.

Daylilies (*Hemerocallis*) have short-lived individual flowers, but new ones are continually

Grasses and perennials with coloured leaves make everything look friendlier.

opening. *Astilbe*, with its white, pink or red colours, creates a fairy-tale atmosphere. *Aquilegia, Hosta fortunei, Campanula lactiflora, Lysimachia punctata* and goatsbeard (*Aruncus sylvester*) are all very much at home in the shade of the woodland edge. Many ferns, grasses and lilies such as the turkscap lily, (*Lilium martagon*), belong in similar company.

Ground-cover plants to keep the weeds down

Extreme conditions don't bother ground-cover plants like ivy (*Hedera*) and yellow archangel (*Lamium galeobdolon*).

In addition to these very low-growing, spreading plants, there are others that can cope with limited space, and will also produce attractive flowers. They include lily-of-the-valley (*Convallaria majalis*), *Waldsteinia, Galium odoratum*, and of course *Geranium*.

Geranium includes many lovely plants that require little attention. Besides producing a generous cover of weed-suppressing leaves, they bear attractive flowers in blue, purple, pink or white. We particularly recommend *Geranium macrorrhizum* 'Spessart', which bears white-pink flowers in May. This is followed later in the year by species such as the salmon-pink *Geranium endressii*, the brilliant violet-blue *Geranium himalayense*, and the wood cranesbill (*Geranium sylvaticum*).

41

Garden design with related colours

A dream garden in pink and violet

The soft colours pink and violet are perfect for sensitive people who see their gardens as oases of peace and harmony. Garden beds and combinations of perennials can create a romantic and fanciful effect, especially if the theme is picked up by the shape of flowers and foliage.

You still have plenty of opportunity to use your imagination, and the result can be a cheerful, youthful look. Flowering starts early with a touch of romance: low-growing pink double tulips 'Peach Blossom', delicate biennial *Bellis perennis* and fragrant hyacinths 'Annemarie', 'Pink Pearl' or 'Lady Derby'.

The pansy *Viola* 'Frosty Rose' is particularly beautiful, and carries on flowering right into the summer — it isn't absolutely necessary to replace it when it's in the middle of its main bloom.

As spring gathers pace, the opening buds of trees and shrubs like magnolia, rhododendron and flowering currant (*Ribes sanguineum*) add their own tones of pink. In the herbaceous border the romance is embodied in violet or pink varieties of *Dicentra spectabilis*, *Hesperis matronalis*, *Saxifraga*, dwarf phlox and *Aubrieta*. Many varieties of *Paeonia* also display shades of pink and violet.

Then comes May, and it's time to add the summer flowers. You can produce some very attractive combinations by mixing the seed of up to twenty different varieties. You can sow them broadcast, like a wild-flower meadow, or you can set out to raise and plant individual varieties. It's important to think about the height you're aiming for: there's quite a difference between plants for cut flowers, which can grow 20-36 in (50-90 cm) tall, and low-growing mixtures which will form a colourful carpet of bloom. Most people plant a considered selection of varieties. The art of 'painting with flower colours' has to be learnt; it takes a little imagination. You won't always get everything right first time, but next year you can build on your experience.

In late summer and in autumn, *Cosmos bipinnatus* conjures up the wonderful shades of pink and lilac. Since, however, the plants are 4-5 ft (120-150 cm) tall, the best place for them is at the back. The spider flower (*Cleome spinosa*) also reaches a conspicuous height. There are lilac or pink sweet peas (*Lathyrus odoratus*) for climbing over fences and trellises, but these can also be found in bush or dwarf forms that can manage without support.

Once the hyacinths and tulips have finished flowering, you can

lift them from the ground (complete with their bulbs) and fill the space that you've made with *Impatiens walleriana* in pastel shades. In full or half shade, you can't beat these long-flowering plants, and they have one more significant advantage: slugs and snails don't seem to like them!

The ideal place for *Verbena* is scattered singly (and very loosely) among the *Impatiens walleriana*, where it rises above the

A group of summer flowers in delicate pastel hues

 If you cut back *Phlox drummondii* after flowering, a second flush of flowers will follow; the display can continue until mid-October. If you take the plants out then, you will have room for inserting biennials such as *Bellis perennis*, which produce their first pink flowers early in the spring.

Annuals and perennials in pink and violet

Agastache mexicana (Mexican giant hyssop)
Agrostemma githago (corn cockle)
Amaranthus caudatus (love-lies-bleeding, tassel flower)
Aquilegia (columbine)
Aster dumosus
Cleome spinosa (spider flower)
Cosmos bipinnatus
Dahlia
Dianthus plumarius (pink)
Godetia grandiflora
Helipterum roseum
Impatiens walleriana (busy Lizzie)
Lathyrus latifolius (everlasting pea)
Lavatera trimestris (tree mallow)
Liatris spicata (blazing star)
Lythrum salicaria (purple loose-strife)
Malva moschata (musk mallow)
Paeonia (peony)
Phlox paniculata
Prunus triloba

carpet of flowers with thin stalks bearing long-lasting, violet-blue or lilac-coloured flowers. Many butterflies will find their way here too.

The tall *Digitalis purpurea* stands high above the flower bed. And if you really like a loose, natural look, you should always make make room for the fine bowl-shaped flowers of the Shirley poppy (*Papaver rhoeas* Shirley series).

 Many of the new *Petunia* varieties are weather-resistant and free-flowering. The Super Cascade series are outstandingly good. Their long shoots make them very suitable for hanging baskets and window boxes, and they also produce good ground cover in sunny situations.

Sunny yellow and orange

Summer comes in with *Tagetes* and *Helianthus annuus*, with *Verbascum densiflorum* and *Rudbeckia*. A garden in yellow or warm orange conveys a mood of optimism, cheerfulness and joy. If that's a bit too much for you, you can give the planting scheme a very elegant note by adding violet-coloured plants (just a few, but effectively placed), and others in green or mid-green, or perhaps tending towards lighter, yellower shades. To give contrasting violet shades in the flower bed, you can plant *Verbena speciosa* 'Fascination', which has a delicate mound-forming habit, or the upward-jutting *Verbena bonariensis*.

Even under an overcast sky, a garden with yellow flowers seems to be cheerful and flooded with light; you can feel the optimism. Yellow makes a very strong impression on the eye, which is why brilliant yellow flowers shouldn't be placed directly next to each other so they cover a whole area — it's better to put them in groups. Yellow makes distances seem shorter, so it makes big gardens look smaller. You can use it rather like a spotlight to highlight individual areas. If your garden's big enough, you can achieve an unusual effect by growing annuals from seed or planting them informally to create bands of colour. Particularly suitable for this are *Erysimum cheiri* or *Erysimum allionii* in spring, and

Tagetes, *Cosmos bipinnatus*, or *Rudbeckia*, which comes in varieties such as 'Green Eyes' (yellow and tall, with a green centre), 'Goldsturm' (yellow-orange–brown), 'Goldquelle' (yellow, double) and 'Goldilocks' (yellow-brown).

Yellow flowers come in every conceivable shade, from the gaudy yellow of *Begonia ×️ tuberhybrida* to the creamy yellow or brownish yellow-orange of *Calendula*. Imagine a

Right: *Golden rod (*Solidago*), sneezeweed (*Helenium*) and French marigold (*Tagetes patula nana*)*

Below: *Milfoil or yarrow (*Achillea millefolium*) and mullein (*Verbascum*) in various forms*

 Flowering plants will always look considerably more effective when they are seen against a background such as a wall, a hedge, or trees and bushes. If your garden has none of these, you can quickly and easily fill the gap by persuading annuals to grow up a trellis. *Thunbergia alata* or *Tropaeolum majus* will provide flowers for many months to come. Ideal for a yellow garden is *Tropaeolum peregrinum* ; it will continue to bear delicate, yellow, exotically fringed flowers until it's stopped by the onset of the first frost.

it looks good next to walls or in terracotta containers. You can get charming variations of colour with plants such as *Gazania*, wind seed (*Arctotis*), *Osteospermum*, and creeping zinnia (*Sanvitalia procumbens*) or *Coreopsis* 'Golden Crown'; these are all bedding plants that can be used to cover larger areas.

Perennials such as *Lysimachia punctata* and *Solidago* spread quickly by producing runners; they're inclined to suppress other plants. *Solidago* in particular needs to be kept under control, but it's very suitable for corners where hardly anything else will grow. The variety 'Crown of rays' doesn't grow more than 2 ft (60 cm) tall; it's a bush form that isn't quite as rampant as the rest.

water-colour painting with a few strong dabs of colour, and you'll be very close to the ideal picture of a yellow garden.

A mixed bed, planted shade-on-shade with perennials and summer flowers, opens up a multitude of possibilities. Pale-yellow *Hemerocallis* in front of a hedge next to *Hosta*, with their leaves in various shades of green, will allow the tall, brilliant-yellow African marigolds (*Tagetes erecta* 'Hawaii') to draw attention to themselves.

Grasses and silver-leaved plants can provide balance. *Chrysanthemum carinatum* and *Calendula* grow and flower luxuriantly, and can be sown broadcast. *Eschscholzia californica* combines a tender and delicate note with a touch of the wild garden;

Annuals and perennials in yellow to orange

Achillea millefolium (milfoil)
Anthemis tinctoria (chamomile)
Calendula officinalis (marigold)
Chrysanthemum paludosum
Coreopsis verticillata
Cosmos bipinnatus
Eschscholzia californica (Californian poppy)
Gazania (treasure flower)
Helianthus annuus (sunflower)
Heliopsis scabra
Hemerocallis (daylily)
Lysimachia punctata (large yellow loosestrife)
Mimulus luteus (yellow musk)
Osteospermum (African daisy)
Rudbeckia (gloriosa daisy)
Sanvitalia procumbens (creeping zinnia)
Solidago (golden rod)
Tagetes (French/African marigold)
Tropaeolum majus (nasturtium)
Tropaeolum peregrinum (canary creeper)
Zinnia (dwarf zinnia)

Refreshing blue and white

Blue, the psychologists say, feels peaceful, refreshing and cool — just right for those hot summer days. Blue gardens look wider and larger, and in the evening the colours seem to blend in a mysterious harmony. White can further enhance this effect by creating a contrast that increases the impact of the various blue tints.

The tall flower candles of perennial delphiniums next to white *Leucanthemum* × *superbum* could almost be a symbol of summer. Cardoons come into flower rather later, but their silvery foliage makes them good companions for blue flowers. White *Iberis* will set off medium-height blue campanulas and lupins to considerable advantage.

It's a pity, but very few flowers have that pure, radiant blue that most people are looking for. Perhaps the ones that come closest to the ideal are the annual forget-me-not (*Myosotis*), *Cynoglossum azureum* and the ground-covering *Nolana paradoxa*. All of these are absolutely essential for any blue garden.

For a proper sky blue, you need look no further than the large flowers of *Ipomoea tricolor*, an annual creeper. Put a support next to it, and it can make a most attractive background to a border; white *Gypsophila* looks very good spreading out below it.

Above: Campanula lactiflora *is the dominant plant here.*

Left: Delphinium, *sage (*Salvia*) and shasta daisy (*Leucanthemum × superbum*) make a harmonious trio.*

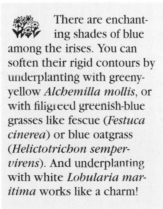

There are enchanting shades of blue among the irises. You can soften their rigid contours by underplanting with greeny-yellow *Alchemilla mollis*, or with filigreed greenish-blue grasses like fescue (*Festuca cinerea*) or blue oatgrass (*Helictotrichon sempervirens*). And underplanting with white *Lobularia maritima* works like a charm!

Summer flowers and perennials in blue and white

Anagallis (pimpernel)
Aster novi-belgii (Michaelmas daisy)
Callistephus chinensis (China aster)
Campanula lactiflora (bellflower)
Centaurea cyanus (cornflower)
Cimicifuga racemosa
Cynara cardunculus (cardoon)
Cynoglossum azureum
Delphinium
Gypsophila (baby's breath)
Ipomoea tricolor (morning glory)
Iris
Lavandula angustifolia (lavender)
Lavatera trimestris (tree mallow)
Leucanthemum × superbum (shasta daisy)
Linum perenne (perennial flax)
Myosotis (forget-me-not)
Nolana paradoxa
Nicotiana (tobacco plant)
Salvia farinacea (farinaceous sage)
Veronica (speedwell)

47

Red: the colour for lively people

Red, the colour of love, embodies sensuality, feeling, activity and the summer.

In June and July, when everything's at its peak, nature sets the trend: brilliant *Papaver rhoeas* edging the paths, *Lychnis chalcedonica* in house gardens, and red roses on trellises and in flower beds.

There can't be many people who will want to do without a brilliant, stimulating red in high summer. Later in the year, feelings change. The year ripens, and the heavier colours become more dominant. In October, we delight in individual signals: the brilliant berries of the *Pyracantha* or the blazing rose hips, which remind us of the warm weather. This is when a delicate pink or violet is the dominant colour among perennials, shrubs and trees.

But the full range of reds has a great deal to offer, from the warm brownish-red of the *Tagetes* variety 'Carmen' to the orange-red of the poppies, from the surprising full red of *Phaseolus coccineus* to the dark red tinted with blue that we see in many rose varieties.

The red shades of *Salvia splendens* catch the eye in carpet bedding, in formal box-edged beds, and in window boxes and other containers. It's often planted with the warm yellow of *Tagetes* or the clear white of *Lobularia maritima* or *Begonia semperflorens*; these

contrasts heighten the effect of the red. Begonias provide any number of variations on the theme. There's a huge selection of varieties among the tuberous begonias: erect or hanging, fringed, some with small blooms, and some with gigantic flowers. They draw attention to themselves wherever they are planted, in containers or in semi-shaded flower beds.

In gardens, parks and flower beds, *Begonia semperflorens* are much-valued long-flowering plants suitable for sun or shade. They have a compact habit, growing into a very smart-looking round shape; they go well in front gardens, by paths, in window boxes and in containers. Different varieties offer a large range of red shades, pink and white. The effect is much

heightened by a combination of plants, white alternating with red, or by plants with foliage of a fully saturated green; brownish-green foliage weakens the effect of the colour.

The red-and-white poppy variety 'Dannebrog' is a real tonic to see. Its colours are in the shape of a cross, reminiscent of the cheerful Danish flag. Similar colour combinations are on offer from the fuchsias, geraniums, petunias and *Impatiens walleriana*.

Brilliant red overwhelms everything when it's planted in large, unrelieved expanses. But red-blooming summer flowers planted in small groups, for contrast, make any flower bed more interesting.

Indian shot (*Canna indica*), for example, conveys an air of

Annuals and perennials in red

Adonis aestivalis (pheasant's eye)
Amaranthus caudatus (love-lies-bleeding)
Astilbe
Begonia semperflorens
Centranthus ruber (red valerian)
Dianthus deltoides (maiden pink)
Eschscholzia (California poppy)
Geum (avens)
Helenium (sneezeweed)
Helianthemum (rock rose)
Hemerocallis (daylily)
Impatiens walleriana (busy Lizzie)
Kniphofia (red hot poker)
Kochia (burning bush)
Linum grandiflorum 'Rubrum' (red flax)
Lobelia cardinalis
Monarda didyma (bergamot)
Nicotiana (tobacco plant)
Paeonia (peony)
Papaver orientale (oriental poppy)
Papaver rhoeas (field poppy)
Salvia splendens (scarlet sage)
Silene (campion)

exotic luxuriance. For companion plants you should consider flowers from more southerly climes, such as the various tobacco plants (*Nicotiana*), or *Heliotropium arborescens*, *Lantana camara*, angel's trumpet (*Datura*) and other container-grown plants.

Lobelia cardinalis grows straight upwards, making it ideal for carpet-bedding, or for more loosely planted beds, where it can make for variety and direct the eye to its own particular attractions.

*Marigolds (*Tagetes*) and scarlet sage (*Salvia splendens*) display strong colours.*

49

Secretive, delicate white

The colour white, embodying coolness, freshness, elegance and brightness, plays an important role in the garden. But virginal, innocent white, the colour of new life, can also stand for the opposite — death. It's fortunate that fewer and fewer people are affected by a superstitious fear of growing arum lilies (*Zantedeschia*) because they remind them of funerals. In fact white garden furniture, trellises and arches increase our feeling of well-being. They suggest a cheerful southern ambience, encouraging a holiday mood and recalling the classical and the modern at the same time. Hardly surprising, then, that the white or silver-white garden is a very popular choice.

White allows darker colours to appear more prominently, especially red and blue. Delphiniums, poppies and red or pink roses glow with even greater brilliance from a group of white *Leucanthemum × superbum*, delicate *Gypsophila* or *Lobularia maritima*.

White is more suitable for semi-shaded or shaded areas of the garden than for those in full sunlight. In these areas leaves with silvery tones show to far greater effect; the colour is produced by the felting of fine hairs. Plants from dry regions grow these hairs to prevent excessive water loss through evaporation.

Senecio cineraria is an excellent companion for bedding plants. The main variety, 'Silver Dust', with its antler-like indented leaves, competes with 'Cirrhus', a newer strain whose shiny silver leaves are only slightly notched but are very hairy. These plants look decorative, and help to balance excessively bright colours. They can be used to edge flower beds, or planted over a wider area for contrast.

A low-maintenance mixture of summer flowers in delicate white

Hydrangea and goatsbeard (Aruncus dioicus) with bush roses in pastel shades

For drier situations, there's a large selection of suitable plants: *Helipterum roseum*, cat's foot (*Antennaria dioica*), wormwood (*Artemisia absinthium*) in tall and mound-forming varieties, bunnies' ears (*Stachys byzantina*), *Lavandula angustifolia*, alpine thistle (*Carlina acaulis*), snow-in-summer (*Cerastium tomentosum*) and *Santolina* are just a few of the best-known.

Herb and perennial gardens planted entirely in white are especially popular in Britain. But among the favoured planting schemes you will always find white or delicate-green striped ornamental grasses such as the indestructible little bluestem prairie grass (*Schizachyrium scoparium*) or *Carex morrowii* 'Variegata'. Even on rainy days these grasses bring colour into the garden, enlivening it and reinforcing the pastel shades of the major perennials and summer flowers.

We really should give more attention to the noble, blue-green leaf colourings; they can transform a combination of only two or three species of bedding plant into a stylish garden event.

For planting in containers with other plants, we particularly recommend the ornamental forms of the herb sage — *Salvia officinalis* 'Tricolor', with its white, green and red leaves, or the distinguished grey-green variety 'Berggarten'.

There's a good choice of white with the summer flowers, too. It's easy to find mixtures of seeds; these should be sown broadcast. They include low-growing species such as candytuft (*Iberis*), annual *Gypsophila*, and white varieties of *Helipterum roseum*, *Lavatera trimestris*, *Helichrysum bracteatum*, *Centaurea cyanus* or *Cosmos bipinnatus*. Sown as a mixture, they will produce a delicate, species-rich carpet of flowers for sunny spots in the garden, and you won't need to be hoeing and tidying all the time. It's also easier to combine these varieties with other plants when you've raised them separately and can plan how to plant them.

Summer flowers and perennials in white

Anemone × *hybrida* (Japanese anemone)
Arabis alpina caucasica
Astilbe
Begonia semperflorens (fibrous-rooted begonia)
Campanula (bellflower)
Carlina acaulis (alpine thistle)
Cimicifuga racemosa (black snakeroot)
Cosmos bipinnatus
Gypsophila (baby's breath)
Helipterum roseum
Iberis (candytuft)
Impatiens walleriana (busy Lizzie)
Lavatera trimestris (tree mallow)

Modern garden design with annuals

The idea of a wild garden has brought with it a change of direction towards a loose planting style, capturing the character of a flower meadow. This same change of direction has also influenced garden design with annuals.

Whether you have round or rectangular flower beds, the pathways, hedges and bushes that surround them all provide a frame that must be filled afresh every year. But despite this, there's still plenty of scope for designing a planting scheme that includes both perennials and summer flowers.

We've already considered the effect of different colours, and some of the ideas that can be developed from them; but it's always interesting to see how those ideas are affecting the direction of new strains being bred around the world.

This phenomenon is very easy to see in the show gardens of Fleuroselect, the international examining organisation of flower-breeders. In 23 different places throughout Europe, experts assess the newest varieties for their value in the garden, and award medals to the best of them.

In the past, strong pure colours and large double flowers were in the majority; nowadays you can find more and more variegated and peaceful colours.

Among *Salvia*, for example, you'll discover parchment-coloured, pink and violet flowers as well as fiery red. With *Impatiens walleriana* the brilliant red varieties are hardly ever chosen, and nowadays violet, lavender, pink, or white with a pink eye are dominant.

The same sort of thing is happening with geraniums, verbenas, lobelias and even with pansies.

This loose arrangement of grasses and flowers looks relaxed and informal.

You can create a harmony of pastel colours in any garden, large or small. And you can introduce some excitement by setting container-grown plants between them as points of emphasis, e.g. *Lantana camara*, standard forms of *Argyranthemum frutescens* or fuchsia, or upright, tall-growing dramatic plants such as beefsteak plant (*Perilla frutescens crispa*), burning bush (*Kochia scoparia*) and *Lobelia cardinalis* or *L.* 'Fan Cinnabar Rose'.

You can plant the beds as broad, island-like, groups of flowers in separate bands, or restrict yourself to low-growing varieties, planted over a wider area. These cover the ground like a carpet, producing a peaceful, unified effect. And don't forget the new varieties that have been bred with a wild-flower character and a loose, filigreed habit.

The fiery-red *Salvia coccinea* 'Lady in Red' and the pink-and-white *S. c.* 'Coral Nymph' are both long-flowering varieties. *Verbena speciosa* 'Imagination' and *V. bonariensis* have an upright habit and grow to some 30 in (80 cm). Like the white-flowering *Gaura lindheimeri*, they are all reliable summer flowers that can lend an air of informality to even the most regimented-looking bed.

Only a few plants are needed to break up the formality of a flower bed or fill an ugly space between the tall stems. Instead

Chrysanthemums create a pleasant contrast with heliotropes.

of the rather stiff, large-flowered *Zinnia* or *Tagetes* varieties, why not choose one of the small-flowered versions?

Ornamental grasses such as the foxtail barley (*Hordeum jubatum*) or feather-top (*Pennisetum villosum*) can also look extremely effective.

You could even borrow a few plants from your herb garden or vegetable plot. The green seed heads of dill or fennel help to soften the effect of tall flowers, while green or red basil can look just as good growing among a collection of brightly coloured flowers.

53

The most important and interesting annuals

Mexican giant hyssop
Agastache

Origin: an aromatic relative of the deadnettle from Central and North America. We grow them as short-lived perennials.

Flowering: The 24–40 in (60–100 cm) tall, candle-shaped, violet, pink or white inflorescences open from June to September, attracting many insects and butterflies.

Use: *Agastache* is suitable for planting in taller groups and as a background plant, and can also be cut and dried. Species that have been introduced are the pink *A. mexicana*, 24 in (60 cm) tall, and the green and violet flowered *A. foeniculum*.

Cultivation: Raise plants by sowing seed in March to April.

Floss flower
Ageratum

Origin: a member of the daisy family with some 30 species in Central and South America.

Flowering: These long-flowering plants bloom from May to October, blue or white depending on the variety. They either form mounds or grow upright and slightly branched.

The strongly scented Mexican giant hyssop flowers over a long period.

Use: Varieties around 16 in (40 cm) tall, such as 'Blue Danube' or 'Blue Mink', suit natural-looking planting schemes.

Cultivation: Raise plants by sowing seed between February and March; take tip cuttings from January to June.

Corn cockle
Agrostemma githago

Origin: originally migrants from the Orient, these flowers were found for centuries as weeds in cornfields. The seeds, however, contain saponins and are poisonous to humans. Now that the purity of agricultural seed has improved, *A. githago* has all but disappeared.

Flowering: finely marked pink blooms from June to August.

Left: *Hollyhocks* (Alcea rosea) *look marvellous in front of walls.*

Right: *Snapdragons* (Antirrhinum majus) *make beautiful cut flowers.*

Use: The cultivar *A. g.* 'Milas' is ideal for naturalistic and cottage gardens, and makes a wonderful cut flower. It reaches a height of up to 40 in (100 cm).

Cultivation: Sow seed directly outside between April and June.

Hollyhock
Alcea rosea syn. *Althaea rosea*

Origin: from Asia Minor and the Mediterranean.

Flowering: The stems are up to 6 or 7 ft (2 m) tall, with rosette-like double or single blooms in many colours, flowering from June until August.

Use: Very popular cottage garden flower for borders, along fences, and for cutting.

Cultivation: Hollyhocks are perennials, but are treated as biennials; sow seed in the summer months (July to August).

Snapdragon
Antirrhinum majus

Origin: Though native to the Mediterranean region, this species has become naturalised

in warmer parts of our country, where it can even survive the winters without difficulty.

Flowering: The shape of the red, violet, yellow, brown or white blooms resembles an open throat. As well as the single-flowered varieties there are several doubles, such as 'Double Sweetheart Mixed'.

Use: Plant low and medium height varieties of bushy habit for use as a bedding plant, and varieties around 30 in (70 cm) tall for cutting.

Cultivation: Sow the seed under glass between February and March.

Fibrous-rooted begonia
Begonia semperflorens

Origin: Many species have found their way from tropical South America to Europe.

Flowering: The colours range from white through pink to deep red. Among tuberous begonias there are also varieties with shades of yellow or orange-red, with a pendent habit (ideal for hanging baskets) and fully double, finely shaped flowers. The new F1 hybrid 'Pin Up' is particularly impressive, with single large white, pink-rimmed blooms.

Use: You can treat begonias as pot plants or grow them in the open in a semi-shaded or shaded place, or in a window box. One of the best long-flowering plants.

Cultivation: You can sow seeds in January or February, but they're difficult to raise: they're as fine as dust, and need a temperature of around 68°F (20°C) and plenty of humidity. They're best in a heated greenhouse. The plants need pricking out twice. They start to flower in May, stopping only in October.

Bidens ferulifolia

Origin: This fast-growing, short-lived perennial from Mexico is a popular container plant.

Flowering: With its little, star-shaped, coreopsis-like golden-yellow flowers 1 in (3 cm) in diameter, and its loose, untrammelled structure, this has exactly the charm and sunny readiness to flower that you expect in a hanging-basket plant.

Use: If you set one or two plants underneath something taller (in a container, or as part of a mixture in a window box), you can be sure of a continuous display of flowers from May until the frosts. You may need to cut it back occasionally, but every so often you'll be able to cut off enough flowers from your window box to make a little bouquet. This hard-working flowerer is also very suitable for naturalistic beds in sunny positions in the open.

Cultivation: Can be propagated from cuttings or seed.

Swan River daisy
Brachycome

Origin: There are around 50 species in Australia.

Flowering: Light to dark blue iridescent blooms from April until late autumn.

Use: *B. iberidifolia* (Swan River daisy) and *B. multifida* have both proved their worth in gardens and window boxes.

Cultivation: *B. iberidifolia* is sown under glass in March or direct outdoors in April. *B. multifida* is propagated from cuttings in January or February.

Pot marigold
Calendula officinalis

Origin: The wild form is a native of Europe.

Flowering: This light-orange or pale-yellow flower brings light and cheer to the flower bed from June until it is stopped by the first frosts.

Use: The breeders have developed varieties with unusual, gerbera-like blooms, including. 'Kablouna' and 'Princess', which have fully double flowers with dark, quilled petals, and 'Fiesta Gitana' with its stocky habit and tangy fragrance. These varieties are better for cutting, look more refined and have firm stalks.

Cultivation: Sow from April to June, in rows or modular pots.

China aster
Callistephus chinensis

Origin: These annual asters do indeed come from China.

Flowering: In late summer. The blooms have many very different forms. There are tousle-headed ostrich plumes, radiant forms, shapes with needle-like quilled petals, ball-shaped peony asters, the thickly quilled princess, the small-bloomed pom-pom and single marguerite asters.

Use: The simple asters have ample supplies of nectar and are visited by many butterflies, The ball-shaped 'Duchess' asters have remarkably firm stalks and all grow to the same height, making them very good for cutting.

We would also recommend some novelties, such as the ray aster 'Starlight Rose'. It's only 12 in (30 cm) tall, with a spreading habit. Among the incurved asters there are some beautiful cutting varieties with firm, smartly reflexed needle-shaped petals.

We may never see a variety that's entirely resistant to aster wilt, because the plants are attacked by completely different pathogens (including *Fusarium* and *Verticillium*). Just before flowering, the leaves and buds start to wilt. Later the stalks and leaves take on a brownish-black colour, fall over and die off. Only preventative measures can help: don't plant asters on a site previously used for asters, and don't raise aster seedlings in garden compost — use fresh seed compost instead.

Cultivation: Sow seed in March or April in trays, garden frames or directly outside.

Left: Bidens ferulifolia *provides cheerful and playful decoration for hanging baskets and window boxes*

Right: Princess asters *have tightly packed quilled petals.*

Wallflower
Erysimum cheiri (syn. *Cheiranthus cheiri*)

Origin: Starting from the Mediterranean, this relatively frost-hardy biennial has spread throughout Europe, not only in domestic gardens but in the wild as well.

Flowering: The sweet-smelling yellow, golden-brown, violet or velvet-red blooms appear in May with the forget-me-not and the late tulips, which are often planted between them.

Use: Wallflowers go well between roses, in flower beds and in terracotta bowls; they grow up to 32 in (80 cm) tall.

Cultivation: Sow seeds between June and August; plant out in final positions by the end of September.

Annual chrysanthemums
Chrysanthemum species and varieties

Origin: These plants come from farmlands bordering the Mediterranean from Morocco eastward to Asia Minor.

Flowering: All annual chrysanthemums have an aromatic scent. They have flat, open, daisy-like flowers and bloom between June and September, sometimes for weeks at a time.

Use: Suitable for bunches of cottage-garden flowers, or can be placed between perennials. Larger unbroken expanses look like a flower meadow.

*Annual chrysanthemums (*Chrysanthemum carinatum) make a colourful flower meadow.*

C. carinatum reaches a height of 24–32 in (60–80 cm) and flowers with marked zones of highly contrasting colour around the dark-brown or black centre. 'Dunetti' mixture has double flowers in white, red and yellow.

C. coronarium, grown as an aromatic-tasting leaf vegetable in the Far East, can be grown here as a seedling crop; it's sold as chop suey greens, shungiku, or garland chrysanthemum. It has white or yellow double flowers.

C. segetum, our corn marigold with yellow flowers, grows wild. The varieties 'Prado' and 'Eldorado' are dark yellow with a dark brown centre; 'Star of the Orient' is light yellow with a darker centre. Height 24 in (60 cm).

C. paludosum is a dwarf chrysanthemum reaching only 10 in (25 cm) in height. You'll know it by its bushy habit and the small, daisy-like white-and-yellow flowers that appear from June to September. It's suitable for containers, for edging, and for low-growing borders. *C. multicaule* is another dwarf variety with golden-yellow, saucer-shaped blooms that flowers from June to September.

Cultivation: All annual chrysanthemum species are easy and reliable to grow. Start them under glass and plant them out, or sow them thinly outside, in rows or broadcast. Sow from March to May.

Cosmos
Cosmos species and varieties

Origin: mainly from Mexico, as well as from tropical and sub-tropical America.

Flowering: They flower for a long period, from July until the frost, with plenty of nectar and pollen for butterflies, bees and beneficial hoverflies. The colours of the delicate saucer-shaped flowers are white, pink, purplish-red or red-and-white striped.

C. sulphureus from Brazil needs plenty of warmth, so tends to perform badly in cold or upland areas. Otherwise it blooms freely between July and September with single or semi-double orange or yellow flowers.

Use: *C. bipinnatus* is a free-flowering plant for borders or cutting, and for wild gardens, too. The variety 'Sea Shells', with its trumpet-shaped petals, is a bit of a curiosity. 'Sonata' has a compact habit, and is particularly suitable for borders; you can get it in white or mixed colours.

Cultivation: Sow seed under glass in March or April, out of doors in April or May.

Pinks
Dianthus

Origin: The wonderfully fragrant pink (*D. plumarius*) has been cultivated from time immemorial. By contrast, the biennial sweet William (*D. barbatus*) comes

from the Balkans and can occasionally be found growing wild at the edge of woodland as far north as parts of southern Germany.

Flowering: There are both single- and double-flowered forms of pink; they've maintained a presence in cottage gardens since the 16th century because they're so undemanding to grow. Most bloom from May to September (sweet Williams flower in June).

Use: *Dianthus* F1 hybrids from crossings with the Indian pink (*D. chinensis*) set the tone for today's gardeners. The low-growing, 8-in (20-cm) high, compact bushes in brilliant colours have proved their worth for bedding and window boxes. The best strains include 'Telstar

Picotee' (carmine with a delicate edging), 'Telstar Mix' (in several colours), 'Color Magician' (with light and dark pink colours on a single plant), 'Strawberry Parfait' (white-salmon with a scarlet centre), and 'Raspberry Parfait', white-red with a purplish-red centre. They're all F1 hybrids, but unfortunately have no scent.

Cultivation: Sow seed in the greenhouse or on the window sill from February to April.

Foxglove
Digitalis purpurea

Origin: The foxglove can be found in woods and clearings throughout northern Europe.

Flowering: In spring, flower stems up to 6 ft (180 cm) tall push their way out of a rosette of very hairy leaves. The conspicuous flowers are purplish-red, creamy-white or pink in colour. The exotically flecked large blooms of the Excelsior hybrids are often particularly beautiful.

Use: Foxgloves look good at the back of herbaceous borders, even in partial shade. You can cut the stems for display in vases indoors, but be warned: all parts of the plant are poisonous.

Cultivation: Sow from June through until August. Foxglove is a biennial, and self-seeds after flowering in June or July.

Today's Indian pinks (Dianthus chinensis) are compact, very free-flowering plants.

Cape marigold
Dimorphotheca species and varieties

Origin: From South Africa, like the closely related *Osteospermum*, *Gerbera* and *Arctotis*.

Flowering: The silkily shining orange-red or yellow daisy-like flowers unfold in June and July. The Namaqualand daisy (*D. sinuata*) likes a sunny spot in a rock garden or border. In damp weather it can last fairly well; in hot, dry weather it's finished in three weeks, leaving other species such as *Cosmos bipinnatus* or *Rudbeckia* to take the limelight. The white or white-violet rain daisy (*D. pluvialis*) is one of the most attractive summer flowers.

Cultivation: You can raise varieties like 'Glistening White' from seed; other crosses can be propagated only from cuttings in late summer or winter.

Livingstone daisy
Dorotheanthus bellidiformis

Origin: From the foggy deserts of Namibia. The narrow, fleshy leaves can store water, indicating that these low-growing ground-cover plants with their long tap roots should be planted somewhere sunny and dry.

Flowering: From June to August; the flowers are yellow, pink, orange, red or white, and open only in sunshine.

Use: Livingstone daisies are ideal for rock gardens, or for use as edging plants or alongside paths.

Cultivation: Sow in April out of doors, or in March under glass.

Chilean glory flower
Eccremocarpus scaber

Origin: This climber from the South American Andes flowers and grows luxuriantly.

Flowering: The clusters of tubular yellow or orange-red flowers, each around 1 in (2–3 cm) long, cover the delicate tendrils in large numbers. The tendrils can be as much as 10 ft (3 m) long.

Use: The Chilean glory flower is a robust climber; it needs full

In this diversity of colour, it's Godetia grandiflora *that sets the tone.*

sun and a little protection. As well as the species, with its orange-red flowers, there are also the 'Tresco' hybrids, which include yellow and red, too.

Cultivation: Start the plants off in the warm; sow in March, and plant out after the frosts.

Californian poppy
Eschscholzia californica

Origin: In springtime in its native California the state's official flower transforms whole tracts of land into a sea of gold.

Flowering: In Central Europe, the flowering period is in early summer, when the plants, around 12 in (30 cm) high, are covered with golden-yellow cup-shaped flowers that close up in wet weather. The buds are covered by a bag-shaped cap which is pushed off when they unfold.

Use: Californian poppy looks good in rock gardens, borders and containers. As well as the yellow-coloured ones, the range includes red (the 'Dalli' variety), pink and violet.

Cultivation: Sow directly where it'll flower, between September and October or April and May.

Treasure flower
Gazania hybrids

Origin: Treasure flowers are natives of South Africa. They are children of the sun, and need a fertile loamy or humus-rich soil.

Flowering: Every plant produces up to 50 flowers. These open from June until the frosts,

Above: *Treasure flowers (Gazania) belong in the sunny parts of the garden.*

Below: *The Californian poppy (Eschscholzia californica) produces a spectacular show of flowers from very little seed.*

but only when the sun is shining; they're impressively beautiful, and the Germans call them 'midday gold'.

Use: Treasure flowers go well in rock gardens, window boxes, borders and containers. You can overwinter any particularly beautiful specimens. The varieties have become increasingly compact as a result of breeding — for example 'Mini-Star' in yellow, orange, white or mixture, or 'Garden Sun' in deep yellow. Despite their rather longer stems and their rather untidy habit, the older varieties such as 'Sperlings Auslese', with their striped flowers, can still have an impact.

Cultivation: Sow in March in the greenhouse.

Godetia
Godetia syn. *Clarkia*

Origin: Godetias, from the rich flora of California and the neighbouring steppe areas, are easy to grow and flower reliably.

Flowering: Silkily shimmering blooms in shades of pink, white or purplish-red are the hallmark of godetia. In a sunny or semi-shaded site, the flowers will appear in July and August; they are very impressive, with stalks around 12 in (30 cm) long, and can also be used as cut flowers.

Use: Godetias have many uses in the rock garden, for borders or as edging plants.

Cultivation: Not difficult — sow direct outside from April to May.

Gypsophila

Origin: *Gypsophila* has its home in the Mediterranean area.

Flowering: Little white flowers on loose branching heads.

Use: Particularly well known are the perennial species *G. repens* (with its creeping, mat-forming habit) and *G. paniculata* (baby's breath). With its delicate white flowers growing up to 32 in (80 cm) tall, this one goes particularly well with roses. The annual *G. elegans* varieties 'Covent Garden' and 'Rosea' (pink) flower from July onwards, and are easy to grow on sandy soil.

Cultivation: Sow thinly in April or May where they will flower.

Sunflower
Helianthus

Origin: Sunflower species grow on the North American prairie, at woodland edges and beside rivers. Best-known is *H. annuus*, also grown for its oil, as a green manure, and for birdseed.

Flowering: The large, nodding, flat flower-heads appear in August, their golden-brown centres rimmed with a thick garland of yellow, tongue-shaped petals. Some varieties, such as 'Russian Giant', grow up to 13 ft (4 m) tall. There are branching varieties and others with expressive single flowers. The main colour is yellow; the range also includes warm shades of brown and red.

Use: Sunflowers are favourite cut flowers; they're good for background planting or for groups. Low-growing varieties continue to gain in popularity for larger pots and for bedding. Examples include: 'Teddy Bear', double, yellow, 24 in (60 cm); 'Music Box', single, mixed colours, 28 in (70 cm); and 'Sunspot', single, yellow, 10 in (25 cm).

Cultivation: Sow in an outdoor nursery bed, or *in situ*, in April or May.

Straw flower
Helichrysum bracteatum

Origin: The straw flower, like many other everlasting flowers, comes from Australia.

Flowering: The flowering period lasts from July to September. Cut the flowers before the firmly structured buds have opened.

Use: Straw flowers are among the most popular cut flowers.

Gypsophila *gives bouquets an elegant, delicate touch.*

They look good in bunches of cottage garden flowers, and their colour range, from white through pink and yellow to brown and carmine, makes them good for colourful borders. Depending on variety, their height is some-where between 16 in (40 cm: 'Bikini') and 32 in (80 cm: 'Monstrosum'). 'Golden Beauty', with its long-lasting flowers and broadly spreading habit, has proved particularly valuable for pots and window boxes.

Cultivation: Propagate 'Golden Beauty' from tip cuttings in late summer or in March. Raise all other strains from seed, sown directly outside in April or May.

Heliotrope, cherry pie
Heliotropium arborescens

Origin: A sweet-smelling plant, ideal for flower beds and window boxes, from the low-lying tropical areas of Peru. It needs warmth to flourish.

Flowering: The violet-blue inflorescences appear from June right into the late autumn. It's entirely possible to overwinter the plant in a light conservatory or greenhouse, treating it like a pot or container-grown plant.

Use: Heliotrope needs lots of sun and a sheltered position. It can easily become stunted in cold areas or continuous rain. That shouldn't stop you from using it as a wonderfully fragrant plant beneath standard forms of *Argyranthemum frutescens* or *Fuchsia*, or as a contrast to yellow in a bedding scheme.

Cultivation: Sow the fine seeds in the greenhouse between January and March. You can also get tip cuttings to root from August to September.

Helipterum

Origin: The *Helipterum* species come from the Australian out-back. After the rainy season they cover vast areas in a carpet of pink like a huge meadow.

Flowering: *H. roseum* syn. *Acroclinium roseum* has flat little flowers, around 1½ in (3-4 cm) across, coloured white or pale to dark pink, with a brilliant yellow centre. You'll see them swaying on their 16-20 in (40-50 cm) long stalks from June to October. By contrast *H. manglesii* syn. *Rhodanthe manglesii* has nod-ding flowers and pointed-oval

Above: *Sunflowers (*Helianthus*) provide nectar and nourishment for many creatures.*

Left: *Blue cherry pie (*Heliotropium arborescens*) makes a good contrast to yellow.*

leaves which wrap themselves around the stalk.

Use: *Helipterum* should be grown for cutting, as it makes some of the best and most long-lasting dried flowers. In rock gardens and wild gardens it makes a magnificent picture planted in smaller or larger patches, just as it does in its native land.

Cultivation: Sow in April or May in warm, sunny places.

Busy Lizzie
Impatiens

Origin: *I. walleriana* comes from East Africa, particularly the island of Zanzibar. The so-called New Guinea hybrids are the result of a cross between *I. hawkeri* and *I. linearifolia*, both natives to tropical New Guinea.

Flowering: The flat blooms are found in all shades of red, white, violet and pink, and all have a long spur. They appear in untiring abundance virtually all year round, in the open, from May until the frost. There are also varieties with double flowers, e.g. 'Double Conflation' or 'Double Blackberry Ice'.

Use: The pink or lavender-coloured varieties are particularly sought-after; they do very well in shady gardens. The best strains grow to cover wide areas. They are very free-flowering and look good in flower beds, window boxes and hanging baskets.

The New Guinea hybrids make beautiful pot and bedding plants for partial shade. The sheen and intense colour of the big flowers, and the firm, shining leaves (some varieties have yellow and green markings) all convey a feeling of the South Seas.

Cultivation: You can raise the varieties 'Tango' (orange) and 'Spectra Mixed' (coloured leaves, several flower colours) from seed under warm conditions in February. You can propagate all the other varieties easily all year round from tip cuttings — they'll even root in a glass of water.

 If your garden suffers from slugs and snails, you should plant busy Lizzies (*Impatiens*). These energetic little plants seem to drive away gastropods while attracting butterflies — in particular the brimstone.

*Busy Lizzies (*Impatiens walleriana*) do well in shady gardens.*

Morning glory
Ipomoea species and varieties

Origin: The splendid morning glories in ornamental gardens come from tropical regions of South and Central America (principally Mexico), and from Africa. These twining climbers help to stabilise their native beaches, and climb like lianas wherever they get the chance.

Flowering: The funnel-shaped flowers are impressively

Lavatera trimestris *'Mont Blanc'* has a bushy habit and plenty of flowers.

coloured white, pink, red or violet. One of the most beautiful varieties is *I. tricolor* 'Heavenly Blue': the sky-blue flowers stay open only until midday.

Among the more beautiful species is *I. purpurea*, which develops shoots up to 13 ft (4 m) long and bears hosts of purplish-red flowers.

I. nil syn. *I. imperialis* climbs up to 10 ft (3 m) high. Its blooms are mainly purplish violet, but there are varieties in other exotic colours. This species needs plenty of warmth.

I. quamoclit syn. *Quamoclit coccinea* (star ipomoea) is characterised by a weak habit. Delicate bright-red flowers ornament this plant, which can grow as high as 6 ft (2 m).

I. versicolor syn. *Mina lobata* is a conspicuous sight with its feather-like orange, white and yellow inflorescences. In a sunny situation it'll quickly climb up to 10 ft (3 m); it flowers very luxuriantly from July until September.

Use: The morning glories will clamber up strings, fences, trees, rose arches or nets, creating curtains of flowers as they do so.

Cultivation: Although you can sow them straight outside, you'll give them a much better start if they begin their lives in the warm. Sow in March, and plant out when there's no further danger of frost.

Sweet pea
Lathyrus odoratus

Origin: This favourite climber comes from southern Italy and Spain. Now it's difficult to imagine gardens without this plant and its delicately scented flowers.

Flowering: White, pink, red, blue and violet blooms. In hot years, the flowering season is over after only a few weeks in either June or July.

Sweet peas prefer cool, damp climates; in these conditions you may still be cutting bunches of flowers in September. Deadhead promptly so the plants can't set seed: this encourages more flowers to form.

Use: Climbing varieties like the long-stalked strain 'Royal' are mostly bred in the cool climate of England and in the USA.

There are also medium-height bushy varieties such as 'Super Snoop' — 16 in (40 cm) tall with long stalks — and dwarf varieties like 'Little Sweetheart', which is only 8 in (20 cm) tall.

All sweet peas are annuals. The related perennial, the everlasting pea (*L. latifolius*), lasts for many years, and grows up to 6 ft (2 m) tall, but its pink, white or crimson flowers have no scent and are significantly smaller.

Cultivation: Sweet peas are sown in March or April, because they germinate best in cool soil temperatures around 50°F (10°C).

Lavatera trimestris

Origin: A mallow from the Mediterranean area.

Flowering: Large, conspicuous funnel-shaped flowers dominate the summer scene between July and September. *Lavatera* does best on sandy, free-draining soils in full sun.

Use: *Lavatera,* long known in cottage gardens, has only won its popularity as a summer flower through the efforts of plant breeders.

Among the best varieties are 'Silver Cup' (pink), 'Mont Blanc' (white) and 'Ruby Regis' (dark pink), all about 24 in (60 cm) tall. They're all suitable both for borders and for cutting.

Cultivation: Sow from April to May in open ground or a garden frame, and plant out spaced at 8-in (20-cm) intervals.

Poached-egg flower
Limnanthes douglasii

Origin: This marsh plant comes from the mountain regions of California and Oregon, where it's damp in winter.

Flowering: Although it's a marsh plant, the poached-egg flower does perfectly well on normal soil. After a short period of growth it develops so many yellow-and-white flowers that the low-growing foliage disappears under them. Leaves and flowers are tender and fleshy.

Use: Sown or planted over an area, they fit well into semi-shaded sites in rock gardens and borders.

Cultivation: If you sow in September, flowering starts in May; sow in April, and they'll flower in high summer.

Statice
Limonium sinuatum

Origin: The garden forms of statice come from the coasts of the Mediterranean, where they also grow as perennials. In our latitudes they're raised as annuals, flowering in the summer months from July to September.

Flowering: Branching stalks rise from flat basal leaf rosettes, carrying tightly packed spikes of flowers with blue, violet, white or yellow crown petals.

Use: These flowers, popular both for cutting and drying, keep their colour for a very long time. They are good for adding a touch of lightness to bedding schemes and between perennials. Butterflies, to coin a phrase, make a beeline for them.

Cultivation: Sow in garden frame or outside between March and April.

Lobelia
Lobelia

Origin: South Africa is home to the lobelia. Among the most popular is the annual *L. erinus*.

Flowering: Their habit is bushy, overhanging or trailing, depending on variety. From May to October little flowers form at the tips of the many thin stalklets, appearing in shades of white, sky-blue, dark blue, pink or violet. Particularly beautiful are the washed-out blue of the bushy *L. erinus* 'Cambridge

Blue', and 'Cascade Mix', a mixture suitable for hanging baskets.

Use: Lobelias are among the most irrepressible long-flowering plants for beds, groups, path edgings, window boxes and containers.

L. × speciosa, the perennial lobelias, were considerably improved by crossings with several species. From sensitive tropical plants came vigorous bushes; with a bit of protection these can even overwinter, producing firm shoots 16-24 in (40-60 cm) long and with expressive flowers. Planted individually or in small groups, they go well in beds of summer flowers; they flower from August to October. Cut, they keep for a very long time in a vase or flower arrangement.

More and more new varieties are proving an asset for the garden owner. Some that have demonstrated their worth are 'Compliment Scarlet' and 'Compliment Blue', both 28 in (70 cm) tall, and 'Fan Cinnabar Rose' and 'Fan Deep Red', both 20-24 in (50-60 cm) tall, bushy and branching.

Cultivation: You need a greenhouse or window sill with temperatures around 68°F (20°C) to raise them. Sow the very fine seed as early as February, so that by May the plants have reached a reasonable size.

*Hoverflies enjoy visiting the poached-egg flower (*Limnanthes douglasii*).*

Left: Limonium sinuatum *'Forever Gold'* won the Fleuroselect Medal.

Right: Lobelia *'Compliment Scarlet'* is well worth trying.

Sweet alyssum
Lobularia maritima

Origin: An annual from the Mediterranean area with a bushy or mat-forming habit.

Flowering: Alyssum are among the most beautifully scented of flowers: a few plants set in window boxes will give off a honey-like scent every evening all summer long, from May until the frost. Encourage new growth by cutting them back. The main colour is white, but there are also less vigorous varieties in pink and violet.

Use: An ideal bedding plant. With its thick mats of bloom, sweet alyssum covers the edges of borders and other edgings, clings fast in cracks between stones and brickwork, and covers the ground between irises and in rock gardens.

There's another important advantage, too: the plants aren't usually attacked by slugs and snails.

Cultivation: Sow in March or April; prick out 3-5 of the fine seedlings together as a clump.

Nemesia strumosa

Origin: One of a South African genus that includes some 50 species. All are distinguished by attractive and brightly coloured flowers.

Flowering: This fast-growing annual plant blooms from June through to September in yellow, orange, red, white and blue. If you cut the plants back immediately after the first flush of flowers, they'll soon produce a second batch.

Use: Some brightly flecked and monochrome hybrids have been produced by crossing with other *Nemesia* species. These are some 10-12 in (25-30 cm) high, and liven up beds and rock gardens in June and July. *Nemesia* also goes well in window boxes and tubs.

Cultivation: You can start raising plants in the greenhouse in March; they'll flower after the middle of May. Outside, sow from April to June.

67

Baby blue-eyes
Nemophila

Origin: These fast-growing, delicate plants are from California.

Flowering: The sky-blue flowers of *N. menziesii* live up to their name all summer long. *N. maculata* is another beautiful species, its open white blooms tinted with purple at the petal tips.

Use: *Nemophila* cast their spell over rock gardens and spaces, in full or partial shade, between perennials, shrubs and trees, or taller summer flowers. They also look good beside a stream or garden pond, and catch the eye when sown in pots or bowls near a patio. Bees are grateful for the rich supply of nectar.

Cultivation: These little plants develop best if you sow broadcast from April to June where they are going to flower.

Flowering tobacco
Nicotiana species and hybrids

Origin: The flowering tobaccos come from tropical America.

Flowering and use: The hybrids of *N. alata* have become popular long-flowering plants. They're around 16 in (40 cm) tall, and in sunny situations they're covered in white, pink or red blooms from June to September. They look good with other summer flowers, in borders, bowls and window boxes.
  N. sylvestris is a pleasantly fragrant flowering tobacco with hanging white tubular flowers,

and reaches a height of 6 ft (nearly 2 m). Its luxuriant growth gives summer flower beds a tropical touch. It looks good with *Canna indica*, *Heliotropium arborescens* or dahlias.

Cultivation: You need a greenhouse heated to 64–68°F (18–20°C) to raise tobacco plants; you can sow seeds as early as February.

Chilean bellflower
Nolana paradoxa

Origin: The deserts of Peru and Chile are home to this annual ground-cover plant.

Flowering: In places where this undemanding plant feels comfortable, somewhere sunny on a free-draining soil, it'll produce a carpet of bell-shaped flowers, sky-blue with a yellow throat, from June to September.

Use: The trailing shoots also make this an excellent candidate for pots and hanging baskets.

Cultivation: Start under cover, sowing in March, or sow directly outside from April to June.

Poppies
Papaver species and varieties

Origin: We find the wild corn poppy (*P. rhoeas*) all over the place in high summer, around field boundaries and on neglected fields. (It's very suitable for wild gardens, too, and in mixtures of field flowers in beds.) The selected form, the Shirley poppy (*P. rhoeas* Shirley series), produces some of the best colours for the border.

Flowering: As well as brilliant red, the single or double mix-

Nemophila maculata forms a carpet of flowers.

*Flowering tobacco (*Nicotiana sylvestris*) combines with cherry pie (*Heliotropium arborescens*) and Indian shot (*Canna indica*) to create a lush, tropical atmosphere.*

tures contain pink and white flowers, all delicately edged. The short flowering period is impressive thanks to the fine colours of the cup-shaped flowers. Their pollen comes just at the right time for many beneficial insects.

Several beautiful varieties of poppy are, strictly speaking, forms of the opium poppy (*P. somniferum*). They include the fully double, cut-petal varieties, as well as single varieties like the red-and-white 'Dannebrog'.

Use: The annual poppies are good in cottage gardens and wild gardens. Unfortunately they only last a few days, or they'd make interesting cut flowers.

Cultivation: You can sow poppies as early as September or

October. That way the plants overwinter and are ready to flower in June. If you sow in March, April or May, they bloom correspondingly later.

Zonal and ivy-leaved pelargoniums
Pelargonium zonale and *P. peltatum* hybrids

Origin: From dry areas of South Africa, which may explain the robustness of these free-flowering plants.

Flowering: Single and double varieties bloom luxuriantly from May until the frosts, and can flower all year round in a conservatory. However, most people bring them indoors when frost threatens and overwinter them somewhere that's as cool and as dry as possible. You don't absolutely have to cut them hard back before winter: provided

they're kept somewhere light, trailing pelargoniums develop more luxuriantly if they're treated gently. Unfortunately it's not always easy to find somewhere indoors that's sufficiently cool and light, so many people now raise them from seed each year.

Use: Pelargoniums aren't just ideal window-box plants, they also do extremely well when planted out in the garden, even in relatively shady and dry situations. There are hundreds of varieties. Brilliant red is still the principal colour, but violet and pink are on the up-and-up.

Particularly distinctive is the weak-growing pink variety 'Rio', with its dark pink eye. Among the trailing strains, the red-and-white 'Rouletta' finds many admirers. 'Mederinum' and 'Enchantress' are among the best-known trailing varieties produced from cuttings, with huge numbers of single blooms in light and dark pink. Summer Showers F1 hybrids are trailing pelargoniums in various colours; you can raise them from seed.

Cultivation: If you've sown the seed early (in December, January or February) at a temperature of 64–68°F (18–20°C), you'll start getting flowers in the middle of May. The best time to take cuttings for vegetative propagation is in August; root them and overwinter them on a well-lit window sill.

*Shirley poppies (*Papaver rhoeas Shirley series*) are simply magical.*

Penstemons
Penstemon hybrids

Origin: North America and Mexico are home to the various wild species of penstemon, which have been crossed to produce today's many large-flowered hybrids.

Flowering: Penstemons have tubular flowers, flared slightly at the mouth, that are long-lasting when cut. The stalks are up to 30 in (80 cm) long, and thickly covered with bright-red, pink or purple flowers with a creamy-white throat. The flowering period is remarkably long, lasting from June through until the first of the frosts.

Use: Penstemons make colourful clumps of long-lasting flowers that brighten up the perennial borders.

Cultivation: Most varieties are winter-hardy, but some are tender. These need to be over-wintered under glass as cuttings and planted out in spring.

Another good use for petunias (Petunia × hybrida) is as ground cover in sunny situations.

Petunias
Petunia × hybrida

Origin: These children of the sun come originally from South America.

Flowering: The original plants had long shoots and lots of little funnel-shaped five-pointed flowers.

Many strains have been developed from them; most modern descendants are F1 hybrids. They produce great masses of flowers, concealing the disadvantage of petunias — that they don't do well in the rain. Even so, it'll only be a few days before the flowers are back in all their glory, releasing a pleasant scent in the evenings. White, pink, all shades of red, violet and sky-blue — all colours are represented, including yellow.

Use: The best forms are the compact varieties with a bushy habit, ideal for window boxes, borders and containers in sunny situations. Several strains (such as the Prio series from the Netherlands) have been developed to combat the adverse weather conditions of northern Europe.

Cultivation: As a rule petunias are sown under glass in February, then grown on for a long time until they're ready to flower in May.

However, some varieties can be propagated only by cuttings. You should root these in late summer and overwinter them somewhere light.

Annual phlox
Phlox drummondii

Origin:Phlox come from the sandy soils of the North American prairies; the cultivated varieties still prefer light, sandy soils and full sun.

Flowering: From June to September they flower in all sorts of colours apart from brown. The flat flowers, around ¾ in (2 cm) across, are borne in clusters on 8-12-in (20-30-cm) long stalks. Particularly pleasing are the star-marked blooms of the Twinkle series, and 'Promise Pink' with its double flowers.

Use: Annual phlox form highly colourful carpets between taller perennials or grasses. They make good edging plants, and also go well in bowls or window boxes.

Cultivation: If the seed is to germinate properly you'll need a greenhouse heated to around 61°F (16°C) in early March, or soil outside that has already warmed up; don't sow outside until the end of April or in May.

Sun plant
Portulaca grandiflora

Origin: As their name suggests, sun plants are eager for sunshine. They come from the broad grasslands of South America.

Flowering: The single or double blooms appear from June to September in white, red, yellow and many intermediate shades. The succulent, fleshy leaves and

Don't sow your annual phlox (Phlox drummondii) too early.

trailing habit indicate that sun plants are tolerant of drought, but conversely they are much less happy in the wet.

Use: In rock gardens, containers, hanging baskets, pots and window boxes these plants radiate southern charm. The double 'Cloudbeater Mixed' is particularly beautiful.

Cultivation: Sow in the greenhouse from March onwards, so that flowering will start soon after the middle of May, or sow directly outside in April or May.

Gloriosa daisy
Rudbeckia species and varieties

Origin: Gloriosa daisies cover meadows, hills and valleys in the sandy prairies of North America. If you have the space, you can try to reproduce this natural

effect by planting larger patches of a single variety in the garden.

Flowering: The variety 'Goldilocks' bears yellow, daisy-like flowers with dark brown centres on hairy leaves and stalks; they open in late summer from August till the frosts. 'Nutmeg' has large yellow and orange-red flowers, and 'Double Gold', with its double yellow blooms and compact habit, is suitable for borders and larger containers. The low-growing, mat-forming variety 'Sonora' is particularly striking, with huge flowers marked yellow-brown.

Use: Gloriosa daisies are free-flowering, inexpensive border and cut flowers.

Cultivation: Sow directly outside in rows in April, later transplanting the daisies to space them 10 in (25 cm) apart, or start them off under cover in a garden frame or greenhouse, sowing at the end of March.

Sun plants (Portulaca grandiflora) are ideal for rock gardens, troughs and hanging baskets.

Salvia coccinea

Origin: A sage species, little-known until recently, that grows wild along woodland margins in south-eastern parts of the USA.

Flowering: Continues uninterruptedly from May until the frosts. New varieties such as 'Lady in Red' (flame-red) and the Sizzler series (various colours) have made *S. coccinea* a valuable addition to the garden.

Use: Compact at first, *S. coccinea* becomes looser and almost filigreed in habit as it grows and branches. As a result the plants fit well into beds of perennials, between roses, grasses, trees and shrubs, where their brilliance will always catch the eye.

Cultivation: Between February and the beginning of March is the time to sow in the greenhouse. Plant out in May once there's no further risk of frost.

Farinaceous sage
Salvia farinacea

'Victoria' was the first variety of farinaceous sage to become popular in borders and larger containers, and makes a useful supplement to the window-box perennials. The 16–20-in (40–50-cm) high plants have an upright habit and branch at the base. As buds, the blue flowers look as if they've been dusted with flour.

Salvia horminum

This species is found wild in the Mediterranean area, and has retained its original charm down to the present day. Its white- or

The dark-blue farinaceous sage is most effective in groups.

pink-veined bracts make it a good plant for borders, wild gardens, wild flower mixtures and beds of flowers for cutting. Height 20–30 in (50–70 cm).

Clary
Salvia sclarea

This old medicinal and culinary herb from the Orient is a magnificent sight. This perennial is often treated as a biennial, sown in summer and planted out in autumn. Inflorescences appear during early summer in the following year, and at this stage it's difficult to imagine what will unfold above the limp, hairy leaves. From June to July you'll see the result: a cloud of light-blue and pink flowers drawing the eager attention of insects.

Reaching a height of up to 5 ft (150 cm), *S. sclarea* is an imposing sight in a sunny position between *Delphinium*, *Achillea millefolium* and flowering shrubs. Once established, the plant always self-seeds.

Scarlet sage
Salvia splendens

It's a big jump from the tropical rain forests of Brazil to the beds, borders and front gardens of Europe, but the scarlet sage has managed it. Its long flowering period, brilliant colours and low, compact habit make it a sought-after partner to *Tagetes, Ageratum, Lobularia maritima* and *Chrysanthemum paludosum*. As well as the popular bright-red forms, there are varieties in pink, white, purple or violet.

Cushion fan-flower
Scaevola aemula

Origin: This Australian plant, always ready to grow and bloom, makes a fast start.

Flowering: The violet-blue flowers, hanging down like fans, continue blooming without interruption as long as enough light and nutrients are available. The plant survives mistakes in looking after it relatively well, and isn't susceptible to pests.

Use: It goes well in window boxes and in larger containers. Given good supplies of fertiliser and water, it branches freely.

Cultivation: Stem cuttings root well in a glass of water.

Butterfly flower
Schizanthus hybrids

Origin: This plant from Chile looks particularly exotic. It's resemblance to the orchids has given it the alternative name 'poor man's orchid'.

Flowering: Between June and August, every one of the 12–16-in (30–40-cm) high plants unfolds a multitude of finely marked pink, violet, flaming red or mottled blooms.

Use: The poor man's orchid is too beautiful to be lost among the crowd in a flower bed. A few plants in a bowl on the patio, in the rock garden or by the path will catch the eye.

Cultivation: If you want to, you can cultivate these plants in pots as well; you can even keep them through the winter as house or conservatory plants. To do this, you need to sow the seed as early as August. Outdoors, sow directly in rows in April or May.

Cineraria
Senecio cineraria

Origin: Some gardeners still refer to this plant as *Cineraria maritima*; it comes from the African coast, and its felted, silvery-white leaves show that it is accustomed to relatively hot, dry conditions.

Flowering: Insignificant little yellow flowers appear after the plant has overwintered.

Use: The total picture of plant and leaves is an impressive one. Cineraria makes a good contrast to fuchsias, roses, dark-leaved dahlias or *Tagetes*, and is a good edging plant for circular, elliptical or rhomboid formal beds. The variety 'Silver Dust' has deeply indented leaves, and 'Cirrhus' displays a pure and decorative silvery white.

Cultivation: The plants need to be started off indoors; sow under glass in March.

The cushion fan-flower (Scaevola aemula) is one of the most rewarding summer flowers, and is also extremely tolerant.

Marigold
Tagetes species and varieties

Origin: Long- and free-flowering plants from tropical Central America and Africa that should be in every summer flower bed.

Flowering: The French marigold (*T. patula*) just goes on producing new flowers, single or fully double, in yellow, orange or velvet-brown, among its sharp-scented lacy leaves. As well as the fully double flowers of the varieties 'Honeycomb' (brown and orange) or 'Goldfinch' (golden yellow), there are single flowers such as 'Naughty Marietta' (yellow and brown). You'll find real floral miracles among the small flowers of the mound-forming striped Mexican marigold (*T. signata*). Varieties include the golden-yellow 'Golden Gem' and the lemon-yellow 'Lemon Gem', both bushy and covered in little flowers.

Use: The huge flower heads of the African marigold (*T. erecta*)

F1 hybrid varieties (the Galore hybrids and the Inca series) go well in bowls or specimen beds. Taller strains for cutting, such as 'Perfection Mixed', have such a strong smell that they're more often used as a striking background plant for the border, or between perennials.

Butterflies are drawn to *Tagetes* as if by magic; so, alas, are slugs and snails. The roots exude substances that attract threadworms (nematodes); they may penetrate the roots, but can't produce viable young after doing so. Use *Tagetes* for biological disinfection in contaminated areas where strawberries, fruit bushes and trees, roses, celeriac, leeks, carrots, beans or dill are growing — it's an effective, natural method of control.

Cultivation: You can sow *Tagetes* directly outside in May, but it's better to start the seedlings off under glass, at a temperature of 64–68°F (18–20°C). That way the plants will be in full flower by as early as the end of May.

Violas
Viola species and varieties

Origin: Pansies and violets have been crossed many times, but the main parent plant is our native wild pansy (*V. tricolor*). At the moment it's enjoying a revival, with more and more new, small-flowered strains.

*French marigold (*Tagetes patula*) above and Mexican marigold (*T. tenuifolia*) below.*

The garden pansy 'Imperial Frosty Rose' comes in glorious pastel shades.

It's difficult to classify the parent plants exactly, though the more compact, small-flowered strains known as violas or violettas mostly come from crosses with the horned violet (*V. cornuta*).

Flowering: Violas bloom from April to October in many shades of colour. 'Johnny Jump-Up' is a small-flowered variety with violet shimmering on a yellow background. 'White Perfection' produces pure-white flowers, 'Bluebird' pure-blue ones and 'Baby Lucia' blue ones with an orange eye, while 'Cutty' has white-violet flowers.

Use: Violas thrive in herbaceous beds, in sun or partial shade. They're also suitable for planting, alone or with other plants, in tubs and window boxes.

Cultivation: By cuttings; some varieties are raised from seed.

Garden pansy
Viola × wittrockiana hybrids

Origin: Mainly descended from native species.

Flowering: In spring (or as early as autumn and winter with some varieties) the many small flowers start to appear; flowering continues into the summer. Pansies like cool temperatures. New strains such as the pale-pink and violet 'Imperial Frosty Rose' adapt better to summer conditions. Apart from the large-flowered Crown series and the

small-flowered 'Floral Dance' in yellow, blue, white, violet and wine-red, new colours add yet more interest to bowls or beds planted with pansies. 'Padparadja' glows with a deep, shining orange, 'Jolly Joker' combines orange and blue, and 'Love Duet' has raspberry-pink patches on a creamy-white background.

Use: Pansies are ideal flowers for winter and spring, with a delicate fragrance and a long flowering period. They work well planted in beds as a backdrop for tulips or narcissi, in window boxes, bowls and tubs, or in bands of flowers in the lawn.

Cultivation: Sow the seeds in high summer (June to August) and try to keep the germination temperature down to 59–63°F (15-17°C). You can do this by covering the seed beds with damp sacking until the seedlings start to appear. Plant out the seedlings in their final positions in September or October, 8 × 8 in (20 × 20 cm) apart.

Zinnias
Zinnia species and varieties

Origin: Mexico is home to some fifteen zinnia species, including a particularly beautiful one that is rarely grown: *Z. angustifolia* has small, bright-orange blooms that cover the ground between taller summer flowers or perennials.

Flowering: Zinnias are available in many strains that come in a variety of different sizes and shapes. Some of them look like carnations, while others resemble chrysanthemums (for example, 'Giant Double Mixed', and 'Thumbelina', which has little button-shaped blooms).

Use: All zinnias make good cut flowers or border plants that grow well in the sun.

Cultivation: Sow direct in rows from April to late May. Precultivation from late March in a greenhouse or garden frame will produce a quicker, more reliable crop of flowers.

An A to Z of the most interesting perennials

Milfoil or yarrow
Achillea species and varieties

Origin: Found growing in many parts of the northern hemisphere.

Flowering: The yellow species *A. filipendulina* is found in many gardens. Its less familiar red and pink relatives come in many shades, grow to 20–24 in (50–60 cm) and have stout stems. 'Cerise Queen', a pink variety, is found in nurseries or garden centres; the 'Summer Pastels' mixture, available as seed, has shades of pink, red, yellow and orange.

Use: These perennials are robust, indestructible and very long-flowering, They flourish on loamy and on light sandy soils.

Propagation: Seed sown in March yields flowering plants as early as July or August. You can also divide the plants.

Left: *White milfoil (*Achillea millefolium*) and the loosestrife* Lysimachia clethroides

Right: *The Japanese anemone (*Anemone × hybrida*) is one of the most rewarding autumn-flowering plants.*

Autumn aconite
Aconitum carmichaelii 'Arendsii'

Origin: Among the many related wild species, known as monks-hoods, there are some from China and others (such as *A. napellus*) that are native to the Alps. All are beautiful and imposing perennials for damp, sandy to loamy soils. They won't cope at all well with drought.

Flowering: The autumn aconite doesn't start flowering until September or October, when its intensely blue flowers appear, borne on firm, straight stalks about 3 ft (1 m) long. Shiny, dark-green, deeply cut leaves add to the impressive appearance of the helmet-shaped

Lady's mantle (Alchemilla mollis) *adorned with pearly raindrops*

flowers, which open in sequence from top to bottom. The plants grow in clumps from thick tuberous roots.

Use: As one of the last flowering perennials of the year, in shady or sunny (but damp) parts of the garden, this aconite is a valuable companion to the colours of autumn asters, *Anemone × hybrida*, grasses, shrubs or trees. It's also suitable for cutting — but note that all parts of the plant are very poisonous.

Also poisonous are the helmet flower (*A. napellus*) — which blooms in high summer to produce loose clusters of flowers on rather frail stalks about 4 ft (120 cm) tall — and *A × cammarum* 'Bicolor', a cross with *A. napellus* that has white-and-blue flowers.

Propagation: *Aconitum* can be raised from seed in autumn or spring. The seed needs to be exposed to cold in order to germinate. The plants can also be divided.

Lady's mantle
Alchemilla mollis

Origin: Lady's mantle grows wild on damp meadowland, for example in Eastern Europe.

Flowering: After a shower of rain, you can enjoy the sight of jewel-like glistening drops on the tips of the wavy-edged, almost cloak-shaped leaves. Lady's mantle makes an excellent cut flower, especially when used with blue sweet peas. It has a delicate fragrance.

Use: Lady's mantle is practically indestructible. It's happy beside the garden pond and in flower meadows, but also in dry situations under trees and between stones. Once it's become established in the garden, it will self-seed, but it won't tend to take over everything.

Propagation: You can sow the seed between September and February. Usually nature will do it for you, providing a host of self sown seedlings. Propagation by division is also possible.

Japanese anemone
Anemone × hybrida

Origin: This hybrid is a cross between *A. vitifolia* and *A. hupehensis* var. *japonica*.

Flowering: In many gardens, autumn is a problem time. The summer rush of flowers is over — so what comes next? Only a few perennials come into flower between August and October. The Japanese anemone is a reliable autumn flowerer. The many round, delicate pink or white flowers swaying on long stalks are popular with insects.

Use: This perennial can grow up to 5 ft (150 cm) tall. It goes well in wild gardens and herbaceous borders, as a single specimen plant in front of trees and shrubs (e.g. rhododendrons), or among the plants at the edge of the pond. Its very long tap root indicates that it can cope well with drought. Buy only plants which have been raised in pots — it doesn't really like being divided or transplanted.

Propagation: It's propagated from root cuttings; you can grow it from seed, if you find any.

Columbines (Aquilegia) have been grown in cottage gardens from time immemorial.

rhododendrons or *Primula auricula* are all good partners.

Propagation: They're often self-seeding, and you can also divide them in early spring or autumn.

Michaelmas daisies
Aster

Use: It's worth establishing several species of Michaelmas daisy in borders and rock gardens. They all flower long and freely, providing a plentiful supply of nectar for bees, bumble-bees and butterflies.

A. alpinus is a native of the Alps, producing expressive, light-blue flowers in early summer. It makes a compact plant, growing 12 in (30 cm) high. In rock gardens and borders, or as an edging plant, it forms thick mounds.

A. amellus is a plant of loose, bushy habit, reaching a height of around 20 in (50 cm). It flowers in the summer, from July to September.

A. ericoides, from the prairies of North America, has been known since 1732. It produces delicate, airy sprays of flowers much loved by insects. Like *Gypsophila*, the little yellow-and-white flowers soften harsh lines and bring darker flower colours into prominence. In the herbaceous border too, *A. ericoides*, about 3 ft (1 m) tall, stays in the back-

Yellow chamomile
Anthemis tinctoria

Origin: This old cultivated plant has become naturalised virtually throughout Europe, where it was once widely used as a natural yellow dye for wool.

Flowering: The flowers are very similar to those marguerites, but in this case they are golden-yellow all over and carried on firm but delicate stems that don't branch very much. They grow to around 20 in (50 cm).

Use: The modest little blooms reveal their magic in the wild garden when they're allowed to spread and flower in large groups, ideally in the company of brilliant red *Papaver rhoeas*, blue *Centaurea cyanus* or white *Matricaria recutita*.
Yellow chamomile should be in every mixture of meadow or field flowers. It's one of the few reliable flowerers that don't fail on sandy or loamy soils, and that can hold their own for many years.

Propagation: Sow from April until October. Flowering starts in July or August and lasts for several weeks.

Columbine
Aquilegia species and varieties

Origin: Granny's bonnets (*A. vulgaris*) has a short spur to the flower, and is found at the edge of woodland; it's a native of Europe. *A. caerulea* and rock bells (*A. canadensis*), with their long spurs, are among the ancestors of the garden columbine.

Flowering: These perennials are 16–20 in (40–50 cm) high and flower in May or June, when they fill semi-shaded and shaded parts of the garden with (mainly pastel) shades of blue, white, yellow, red or pink.

Use: The delicate inflorescences are suitable for cutting. They're an indispensable flower in cottage gardens. Park roses (e.g. *Rosa centifolia* or *R. gallica*),

and the delicate true autumn crocuses (*Crocus byzanthinus, C. speciosus* etc).

Propagation: All Michaelmas daisies are easy to divide. Every three to four years you should lift, divide and replant them. This will rejuvenate the plants and reduce the risk of wilt diseases

Left: *What would autumn be without the indestructible* A. dumosus?

Below: A. novae-angliae *attracts many bees.*

ground, letting roses, *A. novae-angliae* or flowering shrubs take precedence. Grasses and ferns are also good neighbours. Many little flowers appear from August to September.

A. novae-angliae follows later, providing a final blaze of colour in pink, dark red, lilac and white from August until the first frosts. This species grows up to 5 ft (150 cm) tall, and is character-ised by a stiff, upright habit and rough hairy leaves.

A. novi-belgii is a little different, with smooth leaves and a rather looser habit. Its colours tend more to shades of blue, violet and white.

A. dumosus comes into flower quite late on, towards the end of the year. It grows to 12 in (30 cm), and its blue or white flowers harmonise with yellow chrysanthemums, with *Rudbeck-ia* or autumn-coloured grasses, or with the so-called autumn crocuses (*Colchicum autumnale*)

False goatsbeard
Astilbe hybrids

Origin: These plants come from China and Japan. They can develop in semi-shaded or shaded situations as long as the soil is moist enough — if, for instance, it contains some loam. Astilbes can't tolerate drought. If these conditions are met, they're easy to look after, growing in clumps with fern-like, dark-green leaves.

Flowering: The individual blooms are carried in filigree-like loose branching clusters, or panicles. Depending on the variety, the flowers are wine-red, pink, white or creamy-white in colour. Using different varieties, you can prolong the flowering time from July ('Braut-schleier' white, 'Amethyst' violet, and 'Bremen' red) through high summer and on into September. Among the later varieties are 'Cattleya' (dark carmine) and 'Red Sentinel' (red).

Use: The varieties all grow to different heights, and this is helpful because it allows you to create a lively-looking planting scheme with a selection of different varieties.

Low-growing ground-cover plants, *Hosta*, grasses and ferns make good companion plants for *Astilbe*.

Left: Astilbe *in a herbaceous border*

Right: Campanula lactiflora

As long as you have moist soil, you can also plant the creeping dwarf variety *A. chinensis* var. *pumila* alongside the tall varieties. Its furry-looking pink inflorescences flower rather later, from mid-August until September; it forms pleasant, even carpets, which also flower prolifically.

Propagation: You can propagate all astilbes successfully by division during the dormant period.

Bellflowers
Campanula species

Origin: Many species of bellflower are native to this country. These include *C. persicifolia* (with peach-like leaves), the

bearded bellflower (*C. barbata*), the creeping bellflower (*C. rapunculoides*) and the harebell (*C. rotundifolia*), with its round basal leaves. They're all free-flowering and robust, and some of them, including the clustered bellflower (*C. glomerata*), have a tendency to suppress other plants.

C. lactiflora is somewhat better behaved, but can form imposing clumps. It produces numerous delicate blue or white bell-shaped flowers borne on stalks up to 50 in (130 cm) long. They appear when the roses are in bloom. *C. lactiflora* forms a welcome partner to other pink or white perennials such as phlox, *Leucanthemum × superbum* or *Monarda didyma*; it's also good for cutting.

Propagation: By division.

Turtle-head
Chelone obliqua

Origin: The turtle-head comes from the dry prairies of North America. Few plants have as much to offer as this one, and despite its exotic appearance it's completely frost-hardy.

Flowering: *Chelone obliqua* forms thick, compact clumps 24-28 in (60-70 cm) high. The stalks are firm; the pink flowers look interesting and keep for a long time, even as cut flowers.

Use: It flourishes equally well on dry or moist soil, in full sun and in light shade. You won't often find pests on this plant — even slugs and snails avoid it,

A robust, long-lasting and beautiful perennial — the turtle-head (Chelone obliqua)

and diseases are equally unknown. It's well worth giving the turtle-head a try!

Propagation: The turtle-head can be propagated easily, either by division or by cuttings.

Shasta daisy
Leucanthemum × superbum

Origin: The wild ox-eye daisy (*Leucanthemum vulgare*) is found throughout the northern hemisphere. It lends an air of rustic charm to naturalistic borders, flower meadows, house entrances and cracks in walls.

Flowering: *Leucanthemum × superbum* has much larger flowers and a firmer habit. It is particularly suitable for perennial beds and for cutting.

Use: There is a particularly low-growing, compact variety called 'Snow Lady'. This reaches a height of only 12 in (30 cm), making it very suitable for borders of low-growing flowers, for rock gardens and for pots.

Propagation: Either from seed or by division. *Leucanthemum* always tends to spread as the original plants die off, effectively migrating across the garden. The plants need lots of sun, light, air and nutrients, which is why you have to divide and transplant them every two to three years.

Black snakeroot
Cimicifuga racemosa

Origin: This plant comes from the eastern USA.

Flowering: The pure-white inflorescences of the black snakeroot shoot up into the sky like rockets on Guy Fawkes' night. Luxuriant clumps can easily reach 5 ft (150 cm), or even 6-7 ft (2 m).

Use: In a planting scheme of perennials, black snakeroot belongs in the background — it stands out very effectively against walls, palings, shrubs and trees. It also goes well with grasses and roses, or in the area round a garden pond.

Like *Anemone × hybrida*, black snakeroot starts to flower late — the two look good together. If you want to plant shade-on-shade in white, black snakeroot will give the finishing touch to your creation.

Propagation: Increase your stock of plants by division.

Delphiniums
Delphinium hybrids

Origin: Most of the popular varieties are the results of cross-breeding between the European species *D. elatum, D. cheilanthum* from Siberia, *D. grandiflorum* from western China, and various other Asian species.

Flowering: Many varieties have been created. All of them carry single or double flowers on long,

Delphiniums flower twice a year — in spring and in autumn.

erect panicles in all shades of blue, and in pink and white. They flower first in June and July; and then, if you cut them back, they will flower again in the autumn.

Use: No garden should be without delphiniums. They're the ideal partner for white chrysanthemums and red poppies, or for delicate blue flaxes (*Linum*) and pink or white roses. Other good companions for delphiniums are grasses, *Hemerocallis* and lilies, as well as *Lychnis chalcedonica, Achillea millefolium* and *Salvia sclarea*.

Protect your delphiniums from the wind with bushes, screens or walls, or stake them, otherwise the tall panicles may bend over and break. You could become a delphinium fanatic and grow many of the hundreds of varieties available.

Propagation: Many strains from America, like the resilient 'Dwarf Blue Springs' and the Pacific series, can be raised from seed; sow in March, and you'll have flowers the same year. If you need very frost-hardy varieties for a cold or mountainous area, you'll do better with the strains that have to be propagated by cuttings or division.

Fleabane
Erigeron

Origin: The most important ancestors of the sought-after garden varieties — *E. speciosus*, for example — come from the prairies of North America.

Flowering: As early as May and June, these close relatives of the Michaelmas daisy produce their blue, white or pink blooms on slim stalks. The broad clumps can reach a height of 16-24 in (40-60 cm) and are happy in sunny or semi-shaded situations.

Use: *Erigeron* hybrids fit well into cottage gardens and herbaceous borders, and make good edging plants and cut flowers.
The Mexican daisy (*E. karvinskianus*) is sold for window boxes and hanging baskets. This dainty but vigorous plant is often found growing wild in Mediter-

ranean countries, and even in much of England, where it colonises walls and rock gardens. The haze of little pink-and-white daisies appears on the plants for most of the year.

Propagation: By seed, division or tip cuttings. All *Erigeron* varieties are robust plants, and usually survive mistakes in their cultivation without any lasting damage.

Fuchsia
Fuchsia magellanica

Origin: This Chilean species is alone among more than 100 fuchsia species from South America in being sufficiently frost-hardy for our gardens.

Flowering: *Fuchsia magellanica* grows to over 3 ft (around 1 m) tall. It bears numerous small red-and-purple blooms in late summer and autumn.

Use: The plants need a sheltered situation (in front of a wall, a tree or shrubs, for example), soil that is sufficiently moist, and grasses or summer flowers as their neighbours.

If you've ever enjoyed the unending hedges of fuchsia in full bloom in Ireland, you will never forget the enchantment of the sight. But it's not only in the mild Atlantic climate that fuchsias can survive the winter out of doors. If you protect the plants adequately by piling some leaf-mould or peat over them, they can, in time, form luxuriant clumps. They may be cut back by frosts, but will re-shoot.

Winter-hardy fuchsias are characterised by luxuriant growth.

Propagation: By division in spring, after the plants have started into growth, or by cuttings, which should take readily.

Geranium × magnificum

Origin: This splendid geranium resulted from the crossing of *G. ibericum* from Spain with *G. platypetalum* from the Caucasus.

Flowering: Geraniums are among the most robust of perennials, and they never fail to satisfy. *G. × magnificum* is one of the most spectacular, producing huge numbers of dark violet flowers, and with an impressive ability to adapt to different soils. Only very dry, sandy soils make the buds dry out. This geranium flourishes in full sun, and in shade too, flowering in June.

Use: The plants go well in front of shrubs and trees, in herbaceous borders and flower meadows, beside streams and on the pond bank.

Propagation: They are easy to propagate by division.

Plantain lily
Hosta species and varieties

Origin: Plantain lilies are much sought-after for their decorative leaves; they come from China and Japan, where they have long enjoyed the highest esteem.

Flowering: In May, noble foliage rises from thick clumps, unfolding in shades of blue-green, light and dark green, yellow-green or white-green, with a pattern of markings that are often striped, vaulted and ornamentally structured. From June to July, they are crowned by stalks bearing white or blue bell-shaped flowers.

Use: Decorative foliage plants are in fashion, and some of the most beautiful are found among the plantain lilies. They are suitable for shaded sites, where they can be particularly, valuable, providing ground cover and fitting in well with rock garden or woodland settings.

Propagation: It's easy to divide them successfully in autumn or late winter.

Iris
Iris species and varieties

Origin: One of the first irises to be cultivated was the common German flag (*Iris germanica*), which probably came from the Mediterranean. It went on to become one of the most striking and best-known garden flowers of the Middle Ages. The 'lilies' on the coats of arms of kings and princes were probably irises.

Flowering: Throughout the world, these royal flowers have been bred to their present perfection, with thousands of wonderful varieties in every possible colour. The bizarre flowers each consist of three *falls* (petals which hang down) and three smaller, high-arching *standards* (erect petals). Each fall is adorned with a golden-yellow 'beard' in the middle.

Use: Gardeners distinguish between various groups of iris. The so-called bearded irises include: dwarf hybrids for rock gardens and edging; intermediate hybrids around 24-28 in (60-70 cm) tall, whose stocky habit makes them very suitable for herbaceous borders and front gardens; and standard tall strains around 4 ft (120 cm) tall, with branched stems and larger or smaller substantial blooms.

Irises form a remarkably large group. Among the many well-known species are Japanese flag (*I. ensata*), Siberian flag (*I. sibirica*), yellow flag (*I. pseudacorus*), Dalmatian iris (*I. pallida*) with its gold-striped variety 'Aurea Variegata', and numerous bulbous irises such as *I. reticulata, I. danfordiae*, Dutch and English irises and *I. hoogiana*.

Irises do well on dry soils, and also on sandy–loamy or stony ones, ideally in the sun. It's vital to avoid shading the rhizomes with other plants. In peaty or humous soils, too many nutrients or waterlogging can cause rot — though a few such as *I. ensata* can be grown in shallow water.

Plants which go well with irises include *Campanula*, red *Papaver orientale, Linum*, lilies and grasses.

Propagation: By division in the middle of summer, while the plants rest after flowering. Lift the old clumps and separate the viable new growth with a sharp knife. Then place the rhizomes on little mounds so the roots hang down all round, and cover the roots, but not the rhizomes.

Yellow loosestrife
Lysimachia species

Origin: The *Lysimachia* species from central, southern and eastern Europe must be counted among the more robust perennials. They are marsh plants, and produce golden-yellow or white flowers for a long time in high summer. They suffer little signifi-

to a luxuriant display of brilliant-yellow flowers. Creeping Jenny is best known for its capacity to grow rampantly over pond edges in a very short time, so disguising them very effectively.

Another popular species is the white-flowered *L. clethroides* from China and Japan. It has white tail-like inflorescences which bend over elegantly; at around 30 in (80 cm) tall, the plant goes well both near the pond and in beds of perennials, but is very invasive.

Propagation: All *Lysimachia* species can be propagated by division during their dormant period.

Above: *The beautiful plantain lilies (*Hosta*) come in many varieties, often colourfully striped.*

Right: *Many varieties of iris are enchantingly beautiful.*

cant damage from either wet or dry conditions.

Flowering and use: Garden loosestrife (*L. punctata*) has thick inflorescences some 30 in (80 cm) tall. It thrives even under adverse conditions, but can run wild in congenial surroundings. This beautiful long-flowering plant thrives in both sun and shade, and is eminently suitable for flower beds and as a perennial for cutting.

Creeping Jenny or moneywort (*L. nummularia*) can spread over a wide area on moist fresh soils. In June and July it transforms them from a green carpet

Purple loosestrife
Lythrum salicaria

Origin: This well-known wild perennial is a native of Europe, where it is at home in marshes and ditches. These can sometimes dry out, so the plants have learned to adapt very well to changing conditions; they also cope extremely well with variable light.

Flowering: The bright-purple inflorescences can be seen from a great distance.

Use: Purple loosestrife goes well near the garden pond or in a permanently moist marshy area. Even in herbaceous borders, this plant doesn't seem out of place.

Grasses and perennials with pink, blue or violet-coloured flowers make good neighbours, but a full yellow makes an extremely good contrast, too.

Purple loosestrife is of particular interest because it flowers in the autumn.

Propagation: From seed and from cuttings.

Musk mallow
Malva moschata

Origin: Musk mallow is native to this country, so frost and changeable weather have little effect on it. It's at home on sandy soils, but can also adapt to loam.

Flowering: The large, delicate-pink blooms exercise a particular charm — it's hard to believe that plants as pretty as these can be found growing in the wild. Flowering begins in June, and continues right through into October.

Use: In the past, isolated specimens won their way into cottage gardens — they're good for cutting and require little maintenance. The musk mallow shows to advantage in front of walls and in wild gardens, and also in flower meadows.

Propagation: *M. moschata* self-sows readily. It's also easy to raise plants yourself if you sow in April or May.

Purple loosestrife (Lythrum salicaria) *in a pink shade-on-shade planting scheme beside a pond.*

Peonies

Paeonia species and hybrids

Origin: Chinese gardeners already knew about breeding peonies thousands of years ago. These splendid flowers belonged to the Emperor alone, and it was a long time before ordinary people were permitted to see them. The first Chinese peonies arrived in Europe in 1548, where they immediately found enthusiastic admirers, and for a while they took over completely from the native European peonies.

Flowering: Cultivated peonies are either single or fully double: the latter are large and heavy. From mid-June to mid-July they bloom out from clumps that must be three or four years old before they come fully into flower. Native European forms are not so fully double; they have a very pleasant fragrance, and start flowering as early as the end of May. However, cross-breeding has largely obscured the differences.

Use: All peonies love a slightly acid, humus-rich soil; it should be well supplied with nutrients and not too dry. Every winter, these large plants should get a layer of compost around 1 in (2–3 cm) deep, and plenty of water in dry weather. As imposing specimen plants and cottage-garden flowers, peonies are seen to best advantage when they stand alone or in front of trees and shrubs.

Little gems of a very special sort are the moutans or tree peonies (*Paeonia suffruticosa*),

which are immigrants from the Far East. These tender plants need a sheltered situation, and must be left undisturbed for years. This makes it all the more rewarding when the pink, white or cognac-coloured fully double flowers appear in all their splendour on tall, thin stalks up to 6–7 ft (2 m) high.

Propagation: The best time to divide is September to October. Leave each piece of rootstock with at least two or three buds.

Phlox paniculata

Origin: The prairies of North America are home to this particular phlox species.

Flowering: *Phlox paniculata* is one of the most important flowering perennials of the summer; no garden should really

*The moutan or tree peony (*Paeonia suffruticosa*) is a demanding plant.*

be without it. The strong points of this plant include luxuriant, long-lasting, spectacular flowers and a sweet perfume.

Use: *Phlox paniculata* thrives on sandy or loamy soils, which must always be kept sufficiently moist. If the ground's often dry, growth is retarded and the phlox will never reach its normal height of just over 3 ft (around 1 m).

Some plants are weakened by certain nematode worms. This means it's worth looking carefully to see what you're getting when swapping plants; always ask for vigorous varieties in the garden centre or nursery.

Propagation: The plants are easy to divide either in autumn or spring.

Auriculas and primulas
Primula species and
varieties

Origin: The various *Primula*
species come from a wide range
of habitats throughout the
northern hemisphere.

Flowering: The garden primulas
include varieties with particularly expressive blooms, which is
why in the past there were
waves of passionate primula-
collecting. There are still a
number of primula societies left
throughout the world, where
members exchange their plants;
some of the plants are barely
managing to survive, but they
are uncommonly beautiful.

Use: For the rock garden, auricu-
las are rewarding spring-flowering plants with a pleasant fragrance. They really deserve to be
more widely grown again.
  Among the native *Primula*
species are the cowslip (*P. veris*),
a plant of dry, loamy meadows,
and the pale-yellow oxlip (*P.
elatior*), which grows in damp
places in partial shade. These
find a suitable environment in
many parts of the garden, planted between *Galanthus nivalis,
Leucojum vernum, Tulipa* and
snake's head fritillary (*Fritillaria
meleagris*).
  These plants are joined by the
primrose (*P. vulgaris*), originally
a pale-yellow flower. In moist
situations in grass, or among
trees and shrubs, it can spread to
form whole carpets of flowers.
Garden varieties, which come in
a wide range of much brighter

Candelabra primulas love the shade.

colours, cross readily with the
wild form. Wonderful strains
have been developed, with large,
dense rosettes of flowers. From
before Christmas right through
into April, their many colours are
impossible to miss, filling pots
and bowls on the shelves of
garden centres and florists'
shops. Most varieties continue to
develop for some years in the
garden, as long as you look after
them and plant them out when
they've finished flowering.
  There's not enough space here
to do justice to all the many
lovely primula species available.
Of these, the drumstick primula

(*P. denticulata*) comes from an
area that extends across Asia
from Afghanistan to south-west
China. It grows in damp, sunny
places, so in the garden it's at
home near the pond, by steps
and in rock gardens, and also
between roses, sharing with
them a preference for loamy
soils. The dense, globular inflorescences, white, pink and violet,
appear in April.
  Towards the end of May and in
June, the deep-pink cone-shaped

flower spikes of *P. vialii* emerge from clumps of hairy, lance-shaped leaves, growing 8–10 in (20–25 cm) long. At such times this plant looks remarkably like one of our native orchid species. This little gem from China needs a damp place in partial shade, and acid soil. It mustn't be disturbed in spring, because the leaves are slow to appear; don't hoe them up by mistake!

The candelabra primulas — *P. beesiana* (violet) and *P. bulley-ana* (orange, yellow and pink) — have also come to us from China. Both are readily available, and can help create unusual effects with semi-shaded perennial planting schemes, either near water or elsewhere. The loose habit of the inflorescences means that they also fit into wild-garden settings.

The giant cowslip (*P. florindae*) originally came to us from Tibet. Many owners of garden ponds value this long-flowering species (June–September) with its fragrant yellow bell-shaped flowers, which open gradually

on a series of stems 24–30 in (40–60 cm) long. There are also red and orange varieties. All the flowers have a light farina (a powdery deposit). The giant cowslip is a typical pond-edge plant, going well with grasses, *Hemerocallis*, *Alchemilla mollis* and *Astilbe*. It also thrives readily in other semi-shaded situations, e.g. in perennial beds (if they're not too dry), alongside streams and next to trees and shrubs.

Propagation: All primulas can raised successfully from seed or by division.

Ice-plant
Sedum spectabile

Origin: The wild species is at home in dry meadows and screes throughout central Europe and Asia.

Flowering: The varieties that grow up to 12–16 in (30–40 cm) tall, with fleshy stems and grey-green leaves, are among the most important autumn-flowering plants. Their light-pink or

purplish-red umbrella-like inflorescences open up between August and October, in sunny or semi-shaded situations.

Use: The rich supply of nectar attracts crowds of butterflies and bees. For this reason, if for no other, it's important to put ice-plants somewhere where they'll be in full view, near the house or by the pond, in rock gardens, steppe gardens, or in bowls on the patio — in fact wherever you can easily watch all the coming and going. Ice-plants are pretty inconspicuous while they're growing, but from autumn onwards they can dominate the whole scene.

Propagation: The ice-plant can be divided easily during its dormant phase.

Left: *Giant cowslips (Primula florindae) go well with bamboo.*

Right: *The ice-plant (Sedum spectabile) tends to attract lots of butterflies.*

Grasses in the garden

For the most part loose, delicate grasses have one important function in the ornamental garden: they break up planting schemes that are too precise, take the severity out of firm contours, and charmingly reconcile and combine elements that might otherwise not go well together because of their colour or their shape.

Even the more delicate grasses can have a remarkable effect. Besides the shape and colour of the leaves in summer, it's primarily the autumn colouring, with its marvellous shades of brown, gold or red, which ensures another important place for the grasses next to all the splendid summer perennials. At this time of year, when the light is no longer so harsh, their filigreed inflorescences can be seen to best effect.

Annual ornamental grasses

Originally the fast-growing annual grasses were planted for only one purpose: to provide long-lasting material that could be cut for dried flower arrangements. Nowadays the great value of these beautiful plants in garden design has become an important consideration.

Briza maxima (greater quaking grass) from the Mediterranean goes well in wild gardens, rock gardens or by the garden pond. The inflorescences are particularly interesting as they move gently in even the slightest wind. This quirk of nature is even more obvious in the native *Briza media* (common quaking grass or doddering dillies), a perennial that you should be able to find on infertile meadows (with a little luck). Its heart-shaped inflorescences are even more delicate, trembling at the slightest breath.

Coix lacryma-jobi (Job's tears), from tropical Asia, first forms clumps around 30 in (70 cm) high and then goes on to adorn itself with beautiful, silvery-grey seeds. These come in handy for home-made necklaces, and for other crafts, too.

Hordeum jubatum (foxtail barley or squirreltail grass), from Mexico, captures wind and sun with its long, silver, shining awns (tail-like tufts), and brings movement into the flower bed.

Lagurus ovatus (hare's-tail grass), from the Canary Islands, makes rock gardens and flower beds look more attractive. Sown or planted in groups, the silvery-white tufty 'scuts' are real attention-grabbers.

Pennisetum setaceum (African fountain grass) comes from central Africa. It won't survive our winters, so it has to be raised under glass and planted out like a summer flower. During the summer it seems quite unremarkable, but in autumn its inflorescences unfold: they grow up to 3 ft (1 m) high, long, and look a little like bottle-brushes. Whenever the sunlight catches them, they shine with a reddish-silvery

Foxtail barley or squirreltail grass (Hordeum jubatum) *introduces some variety to the summer flower bed.*

light. *P. villosum* (feather-top) can also be grown as an annual, and reaches a height of just 1-2 ft (30-60 cm). It flowers from July to October with arching cylindrical spikes just 4-5 in (10-12 cm) long. Both are strikingly beautiful grasses. They belong near the autumn-flowering *Colchicum byzantinum* and *C. autumnale*, or close to *Aster dumosus* or ground-cover shrubs. Alternatively you can put them among the permanent plants on a patio.

Sorghum nigricans is a grass that very quickly shoots up to over 6 ft (about 2 m). This makes it suitable for disguising unattractive walls or fences; it creates a dark background to borders, against which the delicate colours and shapes of summer flowers and perennials can be fully appreciated.

There are many other ornamental grasses still waiting to be discovered — not just perennials, but annuals, too, which you can raise for yourself fairly inexpensively.

Although nearly all grasses can be sown directly *in situ*, it's worth starting them off under glass at the end of March or in April. With a lot of grasses, it's very difficult to extract the seed from the ears, so (as in the case of *Lagurus ovatus*) they're often sold with their 'tails' on. These can be very difficult to sow.

Ornamental perennial grasses

While the annual ornamental grasses still lead a shadowy existence, you won't find it very hard to get hold of perennial ornamental grasses in garden centres, specialist perennial nurseries or by mail order. Many are also sold in flower shops as container-grown plants.

This has the advantage that you'll know the colour, proportions and shape, and will be able to try for the best effect before you decide the plant's final position. The disadvantage is that plants like these cost rather more, but you can recover from that. More important is the time of year when you plant them: with almost all grasses, it's better to divide them in spring. In autumn they're no longer able to establish their roots properly, and tend to fall victim to winter drought and frost. The root balls are usually tightly matted: don't hesitate to tear them open so the roots are spurred on to further activity.

Here are some of the most beautiful perennial grasses:

Carex morrowii and *C. oshimensis* (Japanese sedge) are planted as a thick cover in semi-shaded or shaded situations. Put them between shrubs and trees such as azaleas, or between tall perennials that only draw attention to themselves in summer. Alternatively you can grow these grasses as permanent container plants.

These beautiful white-and-green striped evergreen sedges, only 8 in (20 cm) tall, don't proliferate. They need a moist (but not wet) soil, and are otherwise undemanding.

Cortaderia selloana, the imposing pampas grass from the steppes of South America, is so well known that it doesn't really need any introduction. Its silvery-white or reddish fronds grow as tall as 10 ft (3 m) in the late autumn. The important thing is to give it a nutrient-rich, free-draining soil, or an application of compost at the rate of 1½–2½ gallons per sq yd (10–15 l/m^2). Protect it against the winter wet by covering it with a thick layer of leaf mould or brushwood.

Deschampsia caespitosa (tufted hair grass) is found throughout the northern hemisphere, and is correspondingly winter-hardy. The panicles grow up to 5 ft (150 cm) tall, from clumps 12–16 in (30–40 cm) high, and in autumn they're coloured brilliant yellow or reddish, depending on the variety. 'Goldschleier', 'Goldstaub' and 'Bronzeschleier' are beautiful cultivars that reach a height of around 3 ft (1 m). You should put tufted hair grass somewhere in the open, so you can enjoy the full effect of its filigreed appearance.

Fargesia murielae syn. *Sinarundinaria murielae* (Muriel bamboo) is a well-known evergreen bamboo from the Himalayan slopes. The firm culms (stalks), up to 10 ft (3 m) tall,

are adorned with narrow lance-shaped leaves grouped in thick rosettes. The stems, which grow in hard, resilient clumps, increase in circumference all through the year, and can become very large indeed. These are graceful plants; all year round they form a decorative backdrop near the pond, virtually unaffected by our frosts, and making very few demands on the soil. However, when you're dividing and planting them in the spring you must make allowances for their energetic growth. If you put in a barrier of plastic or some similar material in good time, you'll be able to stop the bamboo proliferating too much.

Festuca glauca, one of the fescues, comes from the mountains of Central Europe. It's one of the best-known ornamental grasses, distinguished by low-growing hemispherical clumps with blue-green needle-like leaves. The plants look particularly good in small gardens, containers and heath gardens.

Helictotrichon sempervirens syn. *Avena candida* (blue oatgrass) is one of the grasses most often used for front gardens, heath gardens, and in dry and sunny areas. The delicate panicles rising from the blue-green shocks of leaves are at their most effective when they're surrounded by ground-cover plants or low-growing grasses.

Miscanthus sinensis, from China and Japan, produces imposing clumps 10 ft (3 m) high or more. Its unrestrained

growth makes this ornamental grass a popular plant to grow when you need a self-sustaining supply of raw materials. In the garden, the best place for this reed-like grass is in the background or in larger clumps. The silvery-white or brownish panicles don't appear until late in the year; by way of compensation, they make very attractive winter features in hoar frost or snow. This is why you don't cut the clumps back until the spring. There are several varieties with varying heights and habits, and with different autumn colours. Most are winter hardy. 'Gracillimus' forms thick,

brush-like clumps and grows up to 5 ft (150 cm) tall. 'Malepartus', red-brown with red autumn colouring, can grow 6 or 7 ft (2 m) tall. 'Zebrinus' flowers late in the year, and only when the weather has been damp and warm. The leaves stand upright, and are marked with conspicuous crosswise yellow stripes. 'Silberfeder' blooms reliably from August to October with wonderful white plumes; the autumn colour is yellow.

*Fountain grass (*Pennisetum alopecuroides*) makes an elegant display.*

Molinia caerulea (purple moorgrass) is at home in Europe and Asia. The panicles stand loosely upright, growing about 3 ft (1 m) tall, with rust-red or yellowy autumn colouring; they make an impressive sight beside the garden pond or in heath gardens, complementing autumn asters and hostas in their autumn colouring. It's an undemanding plant, flourishing in almost every garden situation.

Pennisetum alopecuroides (fountain grass) is one of the most beautiful grasses for the ornamental garden. The elegant downward-arching brush-like inflorescences begin to look their best in autumn, from September to the start of winter, particularly when sun and hoarfrost show the white or reddish-tinged colours to their best advantage. African fountain grass needs a sunny situation, and the soil must be moist enough; don't cut it back till after the winter. Varieties such as 'Hameln' (2 ft; 60 cm tall) or 'Woodside' (3 ft; 80 cm) are better-looking than the species: both have pleasantly contrasting inflorescences.

Pleioblastus variegatus syn. *Arundinaria fortunei* (dwarf white-stripe bamboo), from eastern Asia, is becoming increasingly popular as a low-growing ground-cover plant. Like all bamboos, its runners spread out on all sides; you can control this by putting barriers of plastic or some similar material in the ground. Apart from that it offers a delightful picture, a thick carpet of loosely arching small leaves, striped yellow and green or white and green. It will tolerate temperatures down to about -4°F (-20°C).

Pleioblastus humilis pumilus syn. *Arundinaria pumila* reaches a height of over 30 in (around 80 cm), with green leaves approximately 4 in (10 cm) long. This is a vigorous ground-cover plant, and you needn't worry about cutting it with the lawnmower in spring in order to prepare it for the new growth.

Stipa barbata, a feathergrass from southern and eastern Europe, makes an elegant sight in late summer with its lightly arching flower plumes. The clumps are narrow, as are the 3-ft (1-m) long green leaves. The plants are suitable for breaking up borders of summer flowers, and for the rock garden.

Other beautiful feathergrasses include *S. gigantea* (golden oats) from Spain, which has clumps 20 in (50 cm) tall and inflorescences up to 8 ft (2·5 m) high — it's a specimen plant, suitable for sunny situations.

Stipa brachytricha is native to Europe, and is one of the most beautiful of the large clump-forming grasses. In the rock or heath garden, it's very suitable for placing alone or in small groups between low-growing summer flowers or perennials. It needs full sunlight and well-drained soil, and produces delicate, silvery or reddish fluttering panicles from August through to October.

Ferns — the perfect companion plants

Ferns are extremely interesting to botanists. This plant group came into existence 400 million years ago, and once dominated the world. Huge tree ferns provided so much biomass that they effectively formed the coal reserves that we can draw on today. Modern tree ferns are tiny compared with their long-extinct ancestors, but we can still see them in warmer countries or in botanic gardens at home.

Ferns don't reproduce by means of seed, but by spores or runners; the latter should be planted in spring.

As they are woodland plants, ferns are ideal for shady situations beneath shrubs such as rhododendrons, hollies and azaleas, or next to ground-cover plants such as ivy, wood sorrel (*Oxalis acetosella*), *Tiarella cordifolia* or *Epimedium*. If you've got enough room, you can also plant flowering bulbs such as *Eranthis hyemalis*, *Scilla*, bluebell (*Hyacinthoides non-scripta*) or *Convallaria majalis* in among the ferns.

Ferns enjoy the woodland humus and prefer a slightly acid soil, though conditions don't always have to be damp. On the contrary, some species such as the male fern (*Dryopteris filix-mas*) can withstand enormous root pressure from trees or shrubs, and manage on the limited reserves of nutrients and moisture that are left for them.

Once ferns are established, they need remarkably little maintenance. In spring they can put on a magnificent display when the delicate green fronds unroll like primeval monsters. But the autumn is interesting too. First the dark-brown sporangia form underneath the fronds, releasing their powdery spores; then the fronds turn yellow or brown.

Propagation from the spores is a challenge, but can be fun. You can germinate the spores on compost sterilised with boiling water. First they will produce small growths (prothalli) on which sexual union occurs,

*The ostrich-feather fern (*Matteuccia struthiopteris*) looks good against wood.*

and after many months you will see new plantlets growing. Runners produce full-grown plants much more quickly.

Here are some of the most important frost-hardy ferns for the domestic garden:

Adiantum pedatum (northern maidenhead fern) from North America is both imposing and delicate in appearance. The 12–20-in (30–50-cm) long fronds spread out into fan-shaped clumps. It would be a pity to let a plant like this disappear into the background. Instead, you should site it where visitors will get plenty of chances to admire this rarity, in the damp shade of walls, on tree-stumps, between low-growing ground-cover plants such as *Tiarella* or *Epimedium*, beside the path or as a border next to shrubs and trees.

Asplenium scolopendrium (hart's tongue fern) is found throughout the northern hemisphere. Some varieties are used as houseplants. All are conspicuously beautiful, with lance-shaped fronds that are lightly waved or frilled, shining, hard and undivided. This plant grows on rocks, in damp upland forests or beside walls — but always in the shade. It also tolerates lime, which makes it suitable for planting beside a stone path, a wall or perhaps a stream.

Blechnum spicant (hard fern) from the northern woodlands has evergreen arching fronds 10–16 in (25–40 cm) long; they're dark green and leathery.

The northern maidenhair fern (Adiantum pedatum) *is a magnificent sight.*

It thrives in very moist and shady situations, close to water.

Dryopteris filix-mas (male fern) is a common sight in woodlands and hedgerows. Like the very similar ostrich-feather fern (*Matteuccia struthiopteris*), it has sterile fronds which die back in autumn, and upright evergreen fronds which are fertile and can grow as tall as 5 ft (150 cm). There are several varieties. The male fern is suitable for planting in wide expanses under shrubs and trees, and among large groups of perennials in the sun.

Matteuccia struthiopteris (ostrich-feather fern) is a popular species in gardens. It grows up to 3 ft (1 m) tall, propagates freely by means of runners, and is undemanding yet decorative.

It will take over shady expanses under trees and shrubs if you allow it.

Onoclea sensibilis (sensitive fern) is from Siberia. The sterile fronds grow to 20–36 in (50–90 cm) in summer before dying back in autumn. The fertile fronds grow to 12–20 in (30–50 cm), but remain standing throughout the winter. This fern spreads rapidly by means of creeping rhizomes, which travel long distances in all directions. Obviously this isn't a plant for small gardens, but it can be ideal for covering large expanses under trees.

Index